The Enneagram for Teens

Discover Your Personality Type

and Celebrate Your True Self

by

Elizabeth Wagele

PLI Media

Published in the United States by PLI Media
PLIMedia.com
The Enneagram for Teens
Discover Your Personality Type and Celebrate Your True Self
ISBN: 978-0-9831995-1-9
Cover design and illustrations by Elizabeth Wagele
Interior design by Red Letter Day Graphic Design
First Edition

Table of Contents

Preface

The Enneagram for Teens introduces you to the nine types of people described by the Enneagram system of personality. Here's an opportunity to discover your own personality type and learn more about your family, your friends, your teachers, and yourself. Adults in many parts of the world already use the Enneagram for help with personal growth, relationships, work, and more.

In adolescence, it's common to bounce between opposites:

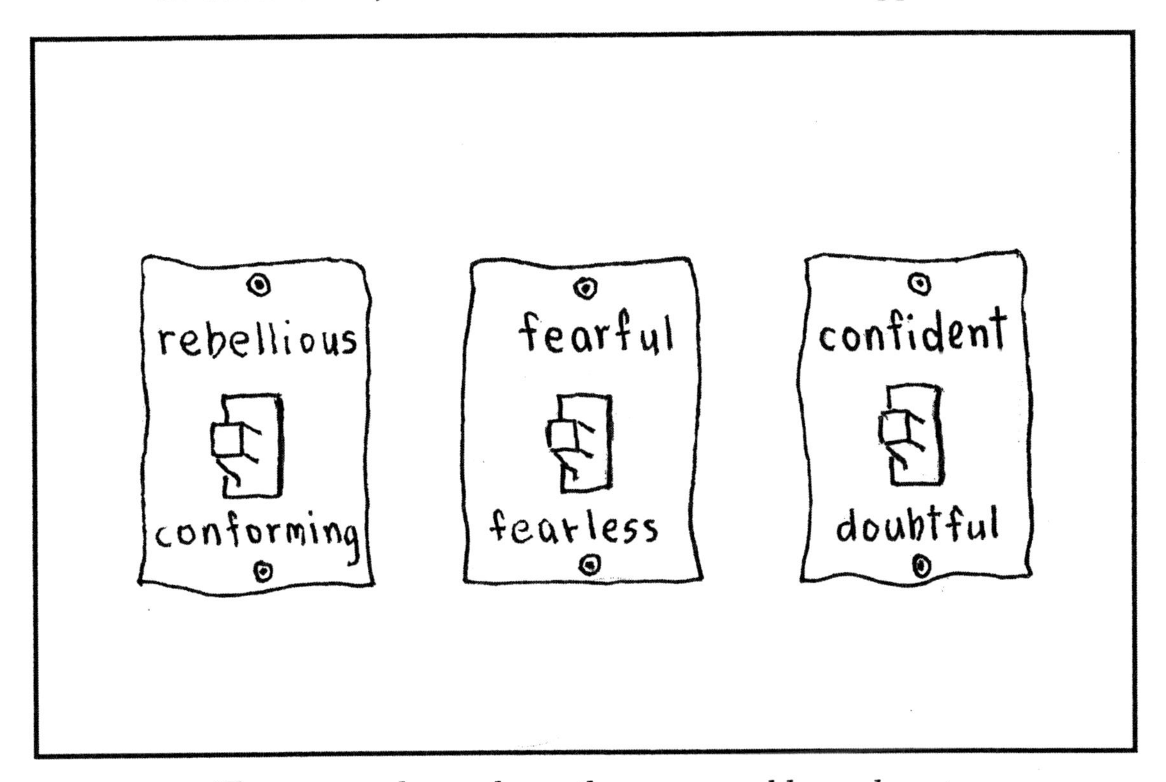

The young always have the same problem—how to rebel and conform at the same time. —Quentin Crisp

I wish I'd had the Enneagram for understanding myself and members of my family when I was a teen. I would sometimes feel angry with my mother for making me do chores, though I later appreciated her teaching me how contributing to the family is an act of love. I would sometimes feel angry with my father for his criticism of my schoolwork, though the skills he taught me helped me succeed in high school and college. I wish I had understood then what motivated me and my parents, and that it is normal to bounce from loving one's parents to being angry with them. I now know it's normal to feel both loving and angry at the same time.

I hope you feel loved and safe in this time of your life between childhood and adulthood. Many adolescents have not been treated well, however, and live under difficult conditions. Depending on your situation, you may:

- feel a pull to stay closely connected to your parents and their way of life
- want to prove to the world and yourself you are self-sufficient
- simply want to avoid pain and feel good

At an age where you may be experiencing many contradictions, the Enneagram will help you find out who you are and teach you how to relate well with others.

Tension is who you think you should be. Relaxation is who you are.
—Chinese proverb

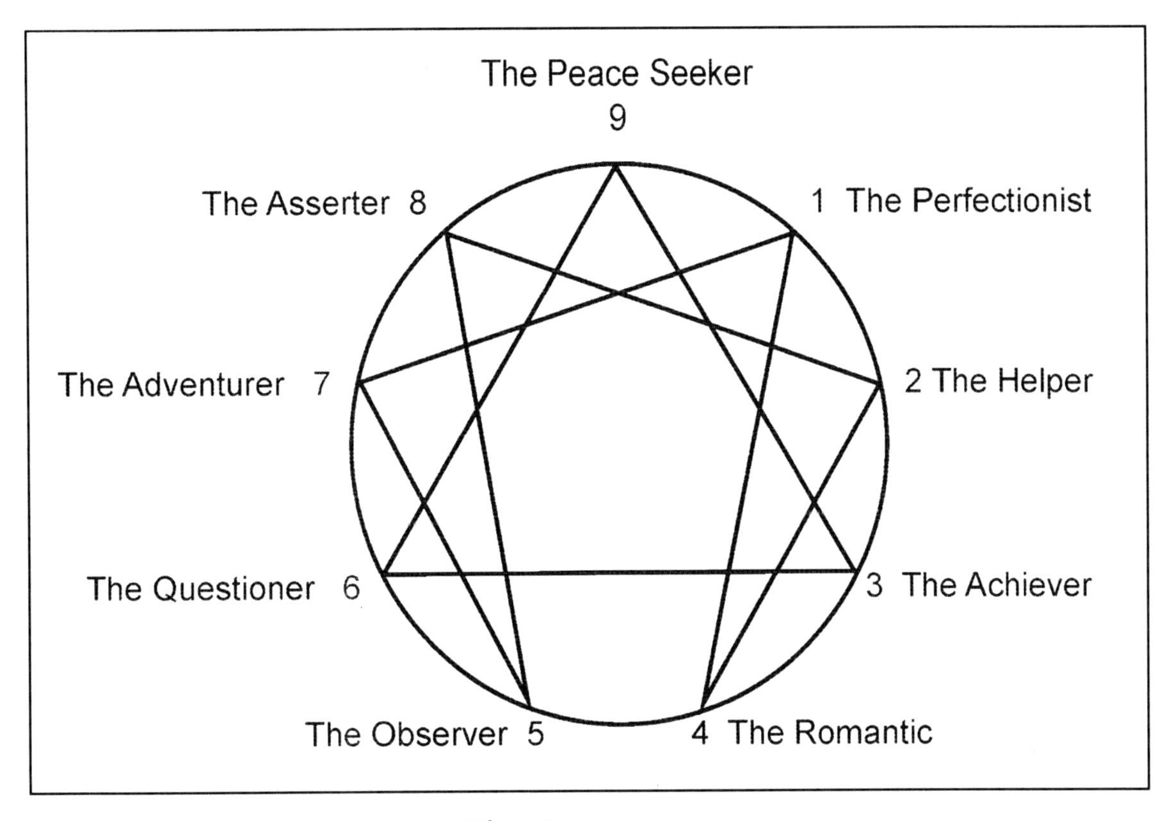

The Enneagram

The nine-point shape stands for the Enneagram system. "Ennea" is Greek for the number 9; "gram" means a drawing. *Enneagram*, pronounced *A'ny a gram*, means a drawing with nine points.

The Enneagram gives you tools to see how your strengths are different from those of your friends and your parents so you can live positively. Are you a gentle Peace Keeper in a family that values being tough and powerful? Are you a poet or musician whom your family doesn't understand, or so tough many don't approve of you? The Enneagram teaches acceptance of those different from us. It has been used to help Israeli and Palestinian youth get along. It has helped children and adults of different races focus on their real differences instead of the color of their skin. It will help you honor what's important to you and learn to express what you want and need.

What is your type?

Answering the questions below will help start the process of deciding what type you are. If you know your type right away, check just one "yes." If you can't decide, check the two or three most likely "yes" options and narrow it down to one after you read all the chapters. Each number matches one of the personalities on the Enneagram circle.

1 – The Perfectionist

Are you orderly and conscientious, and do you tend to follow rules?

Yes __ No__

Perfectionists want to live life the right way, improve themselves and others, and avoid anger.

2 – The Helper

Do you like to have many friends and help others feel happy?

Yes__ No__

Helpers want to be appreciated and to express their positive feelings toward others.

3 – The Achiever

Do you like to work hard and set ambitious goals for yourself?

Yes__ No__

Achievers want to be productive, to succeed, and to avoid failure.

4 – The Romantic

Do you appreciate beauty and think about the meaning of life?

Yes__ No__

Romantics want to understand their feelings, to be understood, and to avoid being ordinary.

5 – The Observer

Do you try to learn as much information as you can about the world?

Yes__ No__

Observers often like to be alone, to be self-sufficient, and to avoid looking foolish.

6 – The Questioner

Do you try to stay safe and/or make sure you can handle whatever situation comes up?

Yes__ No__

Questioners want to receive approval and to feel taken care of. Some do this by being assertive or rebellious.

7 – The Adventurer

Do you make sure you have options and plans for keeping yourself entertained so you won't run out of fun and interesting things to do?

Yes__ No__

Adventurers want to be happy, keep busy, and avoid pain and suffering.

8 – The Asserter

Do you often end up in charge and make sure others don't try to control you?

Yes__ No__

Asserters want to be self-reliant and strong, to make an impact on the world, and to avoid being weak.

9 – The Peace Seeker

Do you like to keep things calm and do you dislike conflict?

Yes__ No__

Peace Seekers want to connect with others and to avoid conflict.

What Each Type Wants

You'll learn more about your and others' personalities in the nine type-chapters from:

- quizzes based on comments by other adolescents
- biographies written by adolescents and former adolescents
- the *seven goals* for adolescents

You and others of your type will discover ways to strengthen each other. The other eight types will model refreshing new ways to behave. For example, I'm a 5-Observer. When I first learned the Enneagram, my 2-Helper friend had certain social skills I was weak in. Now, many years later we've moved apart, yet I still use her as a model for doing things well that don't come naturally to me.

Learning the Enneagram will sharpen your ability to observe. Mary tried not to be overly helpful to her boyfriend when she realized she was a Helper type and he was an Observer type. He doesn't like to be given advice unless he asks for it.

Though you are mainly one type, you'll see how the nine Enneagram personalities also exist within you. Teachers, parents, employers, employees, neighbors, couples, children, and adolescents all benefit from learning the Enneagram.

Real generosity toward the future lies in giving all to the present.
—Albert Camus

Seven Goals for Adolescents

Psychologist Eric Erikson said, "The goal of adolescence is the establishment of a clear and stable sense of self." In each chapter you will be reminded about these seven goals to help you develop habits for living as gratifying a life as possible—now and in the future. The goals are:

1. To develop good work habits.

That which we persist in doing becomes easier—not that the nature of the task has changed, but our ability to do has increased.
—Ralph Waldo Emerson

2. To be mindful of your body.

Learning to be responsible begins here. The next step is to take responsibility for the health of the Earth and the environment.

Do not let what you cannot do interfere with what you can do.
—John Wooden, outstanding basketball coach

3. To be mindful of your social life.

One of the most important personality differences between people is whether you are an introvert or an extravert. Introverts are concerned with their inner world and are likely to have two or three good friends. Extraverts are more concerned with the external world of people and events and are likely to have dozens of friends.

New Golden Rule

When thinking about the Enneagram, keep in mind the New Golden Rule, which says, "Do unto others as *others* would like you to do unto *them.*" (The old one says, "Do unto others as *you* would like them to do unto *you.*")

Pascal married Monica, who soon became ill. He thought the best way to be a good husband would be to treat her the way he liked to be treated—leave her alone and give her loving space to recover. Monica told him she felt neglected, however, and likes to be cared for and pampered when she's sick. Now he treats her how she (not he) likes to be treated.

He who knows others is wise. He who knows himself is enlightened.
—Lau Tzu

4. To be mindful of your emotional/spiritual development.

Notice what you most value about life. Develop your own identity by finding out more ways to feel both connected and separate from your parents, your classmates, and your culture.

5. To nurture your intellect, logical thinking, and problem solving.

This includes making sure your reading ability is good, learning about computers, and doing well academically.

Reading gives us somewhere to go when we have to stay where we are.
—Mason Cooley

You may be interested in the practical and the here and now. It's possible, however, you are a visionary and more interested in possibilities. If you are the former, you learn from the world around you. If you are the latter, you learn more from ideas and theories.

6. To develop interests based on your passions and values.

Following your bliss may or may not lead to a career, but it's important. Expose yourself to art, music, theater, technology, and science. Read, take classes, and get to know interesting people.

Find something you are passionate about and keep tremendously interested in it. —Julia Child

7. To educate yourself on career choices that incorporate your innate strengths.

Typical strengths that might lead you to several possible practical career paths will be discussed in each type-chapter. Which of your strengths do you enjoy most? What jobs can you train for that match your strengths? While going to college isn't appropriate for everyone, more and more employers demand a college education. Take classes in subjects that interest you and/or volunteer at a school, business, or medical facility in the field you're interested in.

Look online. The U.S. Department of Labor Bureau of Labor Statistics http://www.bls.gov/emp/ep_data_occupational_data.htm lists careers with the most job opportunities. *The Career Within You* by Elizabeth Wagele and Ingrid Stabb has examples of careers and a career quiz based on the Enneagram.

If you don't know where you are going, you'll end up someplace else.
—Yogi Berra

Conclusion

You enter adolescence as a child and will leave grown up, however long it takes. You might be older than 21 before you feel like an adult. The most advanced part of our brains, the prefrontal lobe, doesn't fully mature until age 25. Words that describe these years are *change* (physical, mental, emotional), *curiosity,* and *chaos.* You will want something at the same time as you don't want it. Who am I? Who am I going to be? Am I crazy or is the world around me crazy? Do I know my parents anymore? Who influences me? Who do I *want* to influence me—my parents, my society, my teachers, my friends? Aha, my true self, you say, but have I found my true self? I will learn to be my own authority. I will find gifts where I least expect them. I would like a map to follow, but if there is no map, I can live with that.

Don't laugh at a youth for his affectations; he is only trying on one face after another to find a face of his own. —Logan Pearsall Smith

Underneath the change and chaos, what remains constant is that you are one-of-a-kind and your basic personality style does not change. If you had a vivid imagination all your life, you still do. If you've been cautious or daring all your life, you probably still are. You may try many new ways of being during these years, but deep down you are the same basic person when you are twenty-one that you were when you were ten.

Adolescence is a period of rapid changes. Between the ages of 12 and 17, for example, a parent ages as much as 20 years. —Author unknown

Read all nine type-chapters and Chapter 10 on Leadership for perspectives, insights, and ideas to act upon. Some of the stories will remind you that it's normal to feel lonely at your age. The lie about feeling lonely is in thinking you're the only one. Learning about the Enneagram will help you expand your self-knowledge, self-acceptance, and ability to accept people who are different from you.

The Enneagram of High School

Enneagram Type 1 – The Perfectionist

I may have many faults but being wrong ain't one of them.
—Jimmy Hoffa

Part I: Are YOU a Perfectionist?

Ambience: Polite

Attire: Neat at all times

Good at: Being orderly, getting things done on time, doing things right

Good with: One person at a time or groups, depending on whether you're an introvert or an extravert

Noise level: Usually has an aversion to speaking too loudly

Take away: An urge to strive and a willingness to work hard

Influences: Perfectionists are influenced by their wings on each side of their number, the 9-Peace Seeker and 2-Helper. They are also influenced by the two types connected by lines, called arrows. The 7-Adventurer and 4-Romantic arrows can be used for growth, for example when the Perfectionist wants to be more playful (7) or creative (4). See the Enneagram diagram in the Preface.

Perfectionist quiz based on statements by adolescents

How many of these ten sentences do you agree with?

Description

- [ ] I have a strong sense of right and wrong, high standards, and take things seriously. —Darius
- [ ] If my room is ever messy, I can't spend more than 15 minutes in it without starting to clean it. Sam
- [ ] Even the smallest things will bug me, such as a floor with lint all over it. —Sam
- [ ] I'll redo homework if it's not neat enough or I'll clean out our car when I have nothing to do. —Lily

What's the worst thing that can happen to a Perfectionist?

☐ To be a failure in my own eyes. —Darius

☐ To flunk a test or make a mistake that is unfixable. —Sam

What can you learn?

☐ To sometimes settle for less than top-notch work. —Darius

☐ Jamal constantly reminds me that I need to relax more often (he is tired of me making corrections to his grammar). —Darius

How do you keep your boundaries?

☐ I try to stay in control of everything that happens around me, including the people, and still try to be seen as good—so it's not easy. —Curtis

☐ I will get angry, especially if someone violates my principles. —Lily

You're a Perfectionist if you checked more than five of these boxes and identify with more cartoons and interviews in this chapter than in the other chapters.

Famous Perfectionists include: Hillary Clinton, Harrison Ford, Gandhi (idealistic), Laura Linney, and Natalie Portman.

Part II: Being a Perfectionist

These go from youngest to oldest—from adolescents now to adults recalling their adolescence.

Judge Darius

I strive to improve myself and correct my friends. I need to relax once in a while. I am critical of myself and others. Honesty is part of my personality. I'm responsible, capable, dependable and will encourage you to do better. I do my tasks without being reminded.

Ever since I was in first grade, I have been called a perfectionist. I've have high standards for any project I do and won't finish it until it is perfect. All my papers have been fairly neat, but sometimes I get too caught up in an assignment and get mildly stressed about it. I try my hardest to get anything assigned in on time.

To tell the truth, I have been known as a Judge to most of my friends, especially to Jamal. I will compare our assignments of "A" work and push him to do that extra little bit to make it better. Jamal says I criticize him too much. He constantly reminds me "an A is an A," and that I need to relax more often.

Sometimes I feel resentful when others around me don't pull their load. I also need to settle for less than top-notch work. Learning about my personality type was fun and will help me become a better person. —Darius

Sam the Perfectionist

I'm the judge of things done right and wrong. Everything I own has to be in the right spot or else I can't stand to even stay there. Nothing can be crooked. I have such high standards and expectations that most people can't meet them.

Even the smallest things bug me, such as jagged edges or wrinkles in my bedspread. Being a Perfectionist helps me get through my school years by giving me a drive to do all my homework. But there are some drawbacks. A lot of pressure can build up and I try to cram too much stuff into one day. Then I have trouble thinking, which really upsets a Perfectionist.

Being a Perfectionist doesn't mean you can't have fun or play sports. We have a connection to the 7-Adventurer, the type that's good at playing. A lot of times I don't know how to take it easy if I blow a test. So the next time you see a Perfectionist and they just bombed a test, tell them to take it easy on themselves. —Sam

Tidy Lily

I like things neat, orderly, and clear. People who chew with their mouths open really bother me and I am likely to be the only person in the whole world of teens whose room is tidy most all of the time.

I have to have my room looking just a certain way with everything in its place when I go to sleep. I have to butter my toast on the lighter side and when I eat Doritos I look to make sure the cheesier side is facing down. I'll redo homework if it's not neat enough or I'll clean out our car when I have nothing to do. Our house is never messy because I am forever cleaning or straightening up.

When I go to summer camp I clean up messy tables, suitcases, and cabins. My personality is definitely controlling but I like the way I am and I wouldn't change it if I could—much. —Lily

Reasonable Curtis

I get mad at myself when I don't get good grades. My parents are both emotional 2-Helpers. When I was ten, I couldn't stand watching them fight but I tried not to show it. I developed friendships with a group of geeky boys and stayed away from my parents the best I could. I was a slow starter, then in the seventh grade I became interested in science. I went away to college and my parents had a messy divorce. I did well in college, partly because I always got my work done before having fun. I tried to stay out of my parents' business when they tried to drag me in. I avoided relationships for a long time; I didn't want to lead an intense emotional life like my parents did. —Curtis

Responsible Jan

My focus was on being a good girl. I struggled with what that meant to my family, and adjusted my behavior to satisfy what I believed they wanted from me. That usually meant getting A's in school, doing chores around the house without being told, and taking care of my younger brothers. I was often on high alert, as the roles might shift or something might be added that I should know without being told. I found a way to fit the image I had for myself within that structure, however, so I could have a semblance of control.

Following rules

It was different at school. What it meant to be good varied widely, from each teacher, each class, and each student or friend. It could be good to be "cool" and do outrageous things. It could be good to be studious and follow the rules. It could also be perceived as "bad" if I did or didn't do any of those things. Not having a sense of myself outside my internal perception of "good" or "bad" frightened me.

Stuttering and isolating

There were too many ways I could be scorned, not accepted, or wrong. So I ended up shutting down, going inside of myself, and becoming isolated. For several years I stuttered because of my fear of saying the wrong thing. That segued into one school year of not speaking a word because that felt the safest of all. —Jan

Idealistic Diane

My personality was nurtured by my dominating, authoritarian Perfectionist father's standard of "Get all A's." He didn't graduate from high school and wanted us to have easier lives than he did. He also wanted me to meet a man who'd support me. Neither of my parents was capable of real intimacy, however.

Hysterical mother

Mom's parents died young so she had a difficult childhood. She would become hysterical and my father would refuse to minister to her emotional needs. I heard her cry for her mother when I was three years old. I didn't want to be pathetic like I thought she was, so I became competent. I took responsibility for my mother, however, which I resented. She was easy to manipulate and would say, "wait until your father comes home."

Physical abuse by father

I dreaded my father coming home because he'd hit us. When we were older he'd tell us to be home at midnight and he'd mean exactly 12:00. If we were one minute late he'd ground us for a month.

I lived in a raging river of resentment and sometimes a puddle of self-pity.

I had to live under society's and my father's rules, but I could set myself apart. I would say what's good for me is good for me and make my own rules. The whole setup was unjust so I became a rebel and came out fighting. Sometimes I would lie. I could be counted on to do what my family would not approve of.

Idealism

My big cause was injustice—I was concerned about anything unfair. I would always root for the underdog because I felt like an underdog myself in my home. I developed power by winning elections in student government and becoming a cheerleader. I couldn't stand for anyone to be left out. If someone smiled and no one returned it, I would feel sad and be nice to the person who had smiled. This was my way of making things right.

As an adolescent I was reactive, confused, and run by my emotions. I felt different things at different times, and sometimes different things at the same time. I now realize my emotions are fleeting and I'm the same person all the time. —Diane

Rebellious Susan

I don't seem to behave myself as well as other Perfectionists I know. I was a rebellious adolescent. I wanted to find the essence of life instead of cruising along on the surface. I was determined my father, also a 1-Perfectionist, wasn't going to control my life. My mother, a 9-Peace Seeker, was patient, supportive, and often went to battle for me against my father.

I've always loved being organized. I was attracted to art and math in school. My biggest obstacle in art was being too self-critical. Going with the flow was hard. Solving math puzzles gave me a sense of order. A moderate student, I'm from a family of five kids and I'm ruthlessly honest. If my parents liked whom I was going out with, I would stop liking that person immediately. I was attracted to flunkies and hoodlums from poor families. I married someone who was the first real hippy in the area and whose family had alcohol problems.

Anorexic

I dropped out of junior college after 3 semesters and took my college money to live in a Buddhist monastery—my 7-Adventurer desire for experience. At 19 I became anorexic. My first husband brought this on by making remarks about how fat I was like my older brother used to do when I was a child.

Each week, I'd fast for 5 days, then eat for 2, losing about 30 pounds. It took me a while to get comfortable eating consistent amounts of food and even over-indulging at times. Now I realize I wanted to feel light and there are other ways to accomplish this besides starving yourself.

Dyslexic

I'm also dyslexic, which didn't make school easy. Multiple-choice tests confused me and sent me into a tailspin because I would think of too many possibilities. Tests where they told me to read something fast, then asked questions about it, frightened me. A book called *The Dyslexic Advantage* tells the positive things about it.

Alcoholic father

My father had a drinking problem. The only way he could relax was with alcohol. I couldn't accept his enormous flaw. He was also judgmental, hypocritical, and anxious about me. When I made choices that pissed him off he would want to disown me. I was determined to do almost everything he was afraid I might do.

As soon as I found something that interested me I was okay. After I learned to sew in the monastery, I sewed for a store and made patterns (many pattern makers are dyslexic). I loved it.

Unhappy childhood

I wouldn't say I had a happy childhood. Only part of myself was engaged. This was also true at the Zen monastery. When I was younger I'd slump off into a 4-Romantic-like existential depression and wonder what is the meaning of life. In my 30s I found something to get excited about. I have a lot of energy so engaging in something physical makes me the happiest.

Finding meaning in life

My 4-Romantic arrow connection gave me the desire to find meaning in life. I love putting together interesting and subtle plants in the garden and color combinations in my clothing. In aesthetics, I'm not splashy, but not boring either. A lot of thought goes into my subtle aesthetic choices.

My 7-Adventurer arrow gives me the gusto to risk anything to find meaning. People always ask me to do things but I'm already doing twice as much as most people. I'm learning not to be afraid of being overextended. I am healthy, vibrant, and do more than I ever thought I could. —Susan

Part III: The Perfectionist and the Seven Goals

1. **The habit of working hard** (doing tasks around home and routine homework), using time wisely, and good study habits (see #5) often comes naturally to Perfectionists.

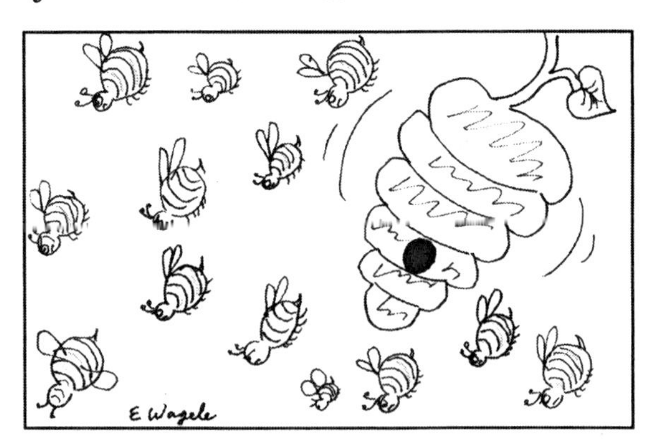

Perfectionists are like busy bees.

2. **Being mindful of your body.** Chances are you, as a Perfectionist, don't have to be told to brush your teeth or to eat nutritious food.

Being happy doesn't mean everything is perfect, it means you've decided to look beyond the imperfections. —Anonymous

3. **Being mindful of your social life.** Perfectionists want to live in a flawless world and to be kind, but they are sometimes overly critical of themselves and others.

4. **Being mindful of your emotional/spiritual development.** Connect to your 4-Romantic arrow to help develop your spiritual side and connect to your 2-Helper wing to help increase your compassion.

5. **Nurturing your intellect.** Perfectionists want to be logical and to know everything they can.

Your Learning Style

- Perfectionists tend to structure their studying and take control of when and where they will do their homework.
- When you study in a group, make sure the leader and group accept all the needs of those present or you may become unhappy. This applies to your classroom as well as when doing homework.
- Stomachaches or headaches are warnings you need to slow down or find ways to lessen your worrying.
- Beware of striving to excel so hard you get too tired or stressed. Perhaps your standards are too high. Consider that good enough is good enough and access your 7-Adventurer arrow to relax and have fun.
- Schedule in some relaxing and fun things to do each day in order to give attention to the parts of your personality that need to rest and play.

Let us read and let us dance; these two amusements will never do any harm to the world. —Voltaire

6. **Develop interests based on your passions and values.** You may be an idealistic Perfectionist who wants to improve the world. Or you may prefer to improve order and efficiency, such as organizing information or the space around you.

7. **These innate strengths may apply to your career choices:** the ability to organize, paying attention to detail, being conscientious, courteous, and fair, and having strong ideals. If these strengths differ from your passions (see #6), develop them both. Your passions will feed your soul while your strengths can support you.

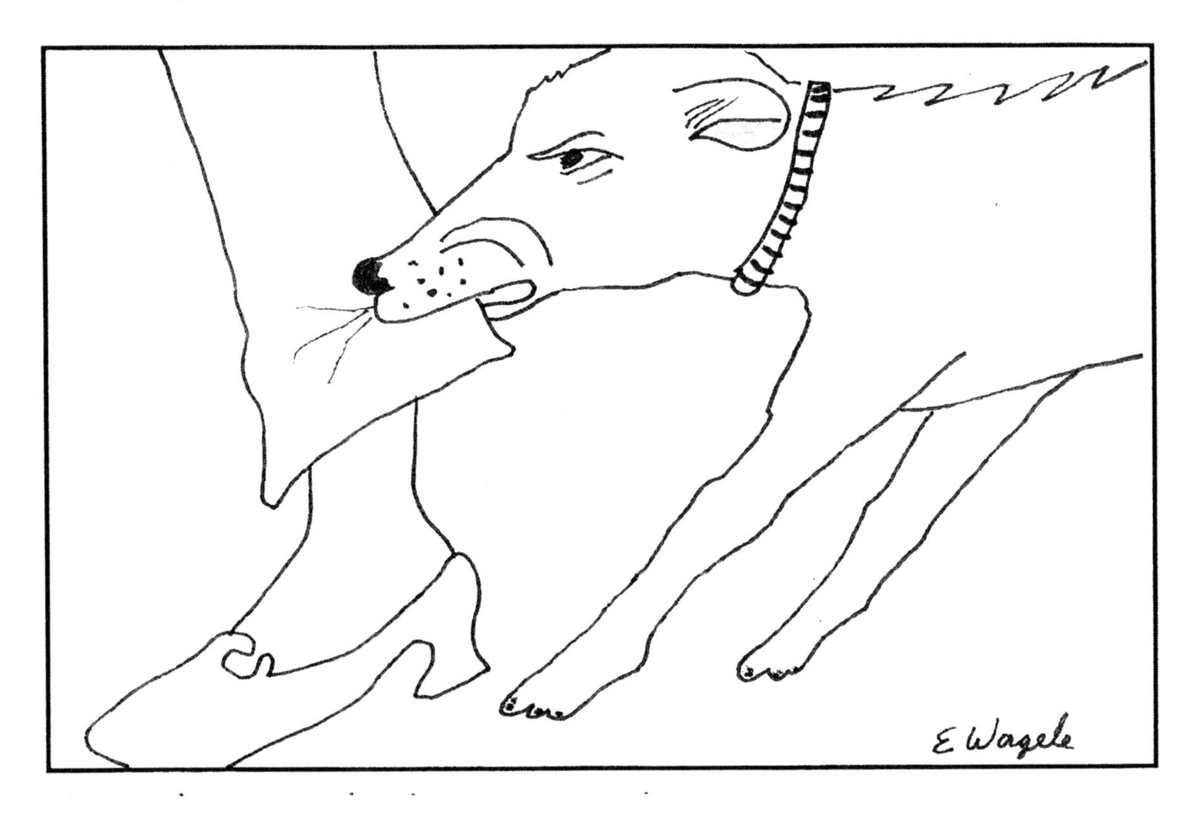

One strength of Perfectionists is persistence.

What interests you—education, business, science, math, engineering, information technology, construction, manufacturing, healthcare, government or non-profit, literature, arts, entertainment, the food industry, the spiritual field, the military, the law, or something else? Whatever it is, you will enjoy doing it the right way and making improvements in your workplace.

Pleasure in the job puts perfection in the work. —Aristotle

Part IV: What I Like about Being a Perfectionist

Part V: Healing Words for Perfectionists

There are two kinds of perfect: the one you can never achieve, and the other by just being yourself. —Lauren King

If everything is imperfect in this imperfect world, love is most perfect in its perfect imperfection. —Gunnar Björnstrand

Everything is perfect in the universe—even your desire to improve it. —Wayne Dyer

Be content with what you have; rejoice in the way things are. When you realize nothing's lacking, the whole world belongs to you. —Lao Tzu

The Enneagram of Adolescence

Drawing from "The Enneagram of Parenting" by E. Wagele. HarperCollins

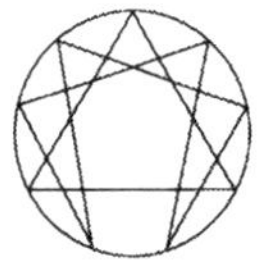

Enneagram Type 2 – The Helper

We are all here on earth to help others; what on earth the others are here for I don't know. —W. H. Auden

Part I: Are YOU a Helper?

Ambience: Harmonious

Attire: Pleasing

Good at: Conversations, giving good vibes

Good with: Children, one-to-one, sometimes groups

Noise level: May be chatty

Take away: A desire to make the world a better place, save homeless animals, help the poor

Influences: Helpers are influenced by their wings on each side of their number, the 1-Perfectionist and 3-Achiever. They are also influenced by the two types connected by lines, called arrows. The 4-Romantic and 8-Asserter arrows can be used for growth, for example when the Helper wants to be more creative (4) or self-assured (8). See the Enneagram diagram in the Preface.

"I'll watch your mouse for you"

Helper quiz based on statements by adolescents

How many of these ten sentences do you agree with?

Description

☐ I love to help people out with groceries or raking leaves. I feel as if I'm a guardian angel for almost everyone. —Precious

☐ I get emotionally hurt easily. —Sookie

☐ I want to be liked and to be part of a group who cares about me. —Sookie

☐ I seek the approval of my parents and try to please them. —Vicki

What's the worst thing that can happen to a Helper?

☐ To be in a place where people don't love me or want me. —Precious

☐ To not be appreciated. —Raven

What can you learn?

☐ I can learn how to not get my feelings hurt so easily. —Sookie

☐ I can learn what I want instead of mainly being interesting in what will make other people happy. —Raven

How do you keep your boundaries?

☐ I wasn't okay during the decade following the plane crash. I put up a wall so people wouldn't know how confused and powerless I really felt. —Elayne

☐ The danger with me is making too many friends and not keeping enough distance. Then I get tired of the person and don't want to be their friend any more. —Precious

You're a Helper if you checked more than five of these boxes and identify with more cartoons and interviews in this chapter than in the other chapters.

Famous Helpers include: Christina Aguilera, Juliette Binoche, Celine Dion, Christina Hendricks, Mariah Carey, and Jennifer Lopez.

The trouble with being punctual is that no one is there to appreciate it.

Part II: Being a Helper

These go from youngest to oldest—from adolescents now to adults recalling their adolescence.

Precious the Nurturer

I'm a giver, caretaker, and nurturer; I give lots of love and want love and I'm interested in how I look. Types 2, 3 and 4 are the most interested in their image or how they look to others.

If someone needs another person to talk to, I can tell and am waiting. I had a next-door neighbor who was 70 years old. It would snow all the time in the winter and I helped her shovel her driveway. My other next-door neighbor was an old humbug, a greedy old man who only loved his dog and wife! I went to his house one evening and gave him a little basketful of goodies. He was so happy he gave me a gift in return. I feel good for being generous and doing good things for people. I also love to have fun. —Precious

You give but little when you give of your possessions. It is when you truly give of yourself that you truly give. —Kahlil Gibran

Raven and Appreciation

It feels bad to not be appreciated because I work hard to help people and I like to be liked. This incident helped me know for sure I was a Helper: my step-dad was sleeping and my little sister and big and little brother needed to have dinner, so I made my brothers pizza and my sister Spaghetti-o's. I also went through the trouble of making my step-dad and me raviolis with good sauce and no one said thank you. I was soooo mad I felt verrrry unappreciated.

I connected right away when I heard Twos are caregivers. – Raven

Kind Person Sookie

I want to be liked and to be part of a group who cares about me. I feel really sad if an animal dies on a TV show. We all have feelings but we Helpers have a weakness. I get emotionally hurt easily and have a hard time dealing with people who think I'm too demanding.

Most Helpers have an easy time making friends but I don't. I only have two real friends but that's okay. I'll try to make more. I like a lot of people but I'm not sure they like me and I'm too chicken to hang out with them in fear they will make fun of me.

I like to be nice. I'm a people person. I want most to have a deep relationship with a friend. Having caring friends and family is all that matters to me. I'm just not good at making the right friends. —Sookie

Hap and Boarding School

When I was 13 I went to live at boarding school. Rowing was important there. I was homesick and scared at first. I took up rowing and in a few years made the varsity team because I could do it and I was tall. This helped my social life. I also got good grades.

Everybody had a job and the seniors would inspect. We had quiet study halls with a teacher who was famous for teaching study habits.

Sometimes I would feel good and sometimes I would feel bad. Who I thought I was kept changing, like an ongoing stream of varying thoughts and moods. In a way, there was no such thing as a stationary "me." —Hap

Elayne's Tragedy

I was the go-between and caretaker in my family when I was a child. But I didn't do a very good job of taking care of myself. I've always taken things personally. If someone looked at me sideways or said something like "What makes you think that?" I'd get my feelings hurt and burst into tears. I wish a book on overcoming rejection had been available to me years ago; maybe I wouldn't have accumulated so many dings and dents along the rejection road.

Tragedy

And what a bumpy road it was – when I was twelve years old my mother and grandmother died in a plane crash, leaving my father to care for me and my younger brother, Lee.

Drawing from "The Enneagram of Death" by E. Wagele. IEA

We moved a lot – from Washington, DC, to Omaha, Nebraska, to Baltimore, Maryland (just in time for my senior year of high school), to Tuscaloosa. Moving my senior year was the hardest; I had worked really hard for the yearbook and newspaper positions and giving up being cheerleading captain really hurt. I had to leave old friends, start a new school, learn new routines, adjust to a step-family, and make new friends. And in Baltimore the social rules were so different and confused me. I felt as if I were on the outside looking in, as if I didn't belong anywhere.

Feeling left out

For me, feeling left out is connected to feeling different from other people. Both of these feelings are linked to the loss of my mother and grandmother. I floated through middle school and high school. Everything was surreal. I don't remember much about those years. But some memories are vivid: Right after the accident happened, I was walking across the field at school and a group of girls suddenly stopped talking. I just knew they were talking about me, feeling sorry for me. But no one knew what to say. I wasn't okay during the decade following the plane crash. My brother Lee wasn't okay. I put up a wall so people wouldn't know how confused and powerless I felt. I never talked about the crash to anyone, even my best friends. —Elayne

Vicki's Unusual Family

I hated to disappoint or hear the word no. It frightened me so I wouldn't even ask the question. I didn't have it in me to rebel or stir up the pot. I wanted to please my parents and seek their approval.

Vicki

Divorce and alcoholic/gay stepmother

During my adolescence my parents got divorced and my mother was in a relationship with another woman. Kids would ask if she was a lesbian but I never asked my mother about it. I didn't have the courage and didn't want to make her uncomfortable. The other woman was an alcoholic. I tried not to upset her when she was drunk and would spend those nights at friends' houses. I dressed younger than my age and was a late bloomer. I wouldn't ask for help with homework. The good times were when we went out to a restaurant with the family.

A boy would visit me and bring me candy. I found out years later that his mother was also a lesbian. —Vicki

Part III: The Helper and the Seven Goals

1. **Developing the habits of using time wisely and studying effectively** (see #5). Make sure you feel good in your surroundings. If anything interferes with good work habits, a likely reason is being overly interested in your social life.
2. **Being mindful your body.** As a 2, you probably already pay attention to looking attractive.
3. **You likely are already being mindful of your social life.** As a Helper, it's important to seek positive, meaningful relationships.

Henry realized nobody can be perfectly likable and perfectly real at the same time so he tried to be honest and real. He also found it was impossible to be fair, kind, cool, in-control, funny, generous, and liked by everyone 100% of the time.

Most adolescents of your generation are connected with more people than in your parents' generation—through social media, texting and e-mail. At the same time, however, most of your generation do not spend as much time socializing face-to-face.

4. **Paying attention to your emotional and spiritual development.** Use your 4-Romantic arrow and do creative projects to nurture your emotional and spiritual sides. Consider focusing more attention on your inner life instead of on other people. Becoming involved in creative projects is helpful for your type.

5. **Nurturing your intellect.**

We read to know we are not alone. —C. S. Lewis

Your Learning Style

- Some of you are decisive and structured. Other 2's are more laid back and flexible. As a Helper, you are likely to be a feeling type and interested in learning about other people through personal stories.
- When you study, make sure you are in a pleasing environment.
- Others in a class or study group may ask you for help and it may be difficult for you to refuse them. Remember you are there for your own learning, however, and be willing to say no.
- Be careful not to take criticism or feedback personally.
- Beware of the tendency to want to make new friends or talk to friends you already have instead of concentrating on learning in class. Do your

homework right after school to make sure it gets done and socialize afterward.

6. **Developing interests based on your passions and values.** Allow yourself to take up other interests in addition to people, for example chess, art, solo sports, computers, math and so on.

One of my passions

7. **Educate yourself about career choices** that incorporate your innate strengths of caring, creating a feel-good atmosphere, going the extra mile, creativity centered on relationships, having excellent people skills, and being tuned in to people's needs. If these strengths differ from your passions (see #6), for practical reasons develop these strengths at the same time as you pursue your passions. Your passions will feed your soul while your strengths will support you financially.

What interests you—teaching, the medical field, business, literature, arts, entertainment, science, information technology, the law, government, commerce, religion, or something else? Whatever it is, you will probably enjoy your skills working with or near people.

Part IV: What I Like about being a Helper

Part V: Healing Words for Helpers

Never give up your quest to find true love starting with loving yourself.
—Alan Cohen

Be careful of the friends you choose for you will become like them.
—W. Clement Stone

True love is no game of the faint-hearted and the weak.
It is born of strength and understanding.
—Meher Baba

Appreciation is a wonderful thing: It makes what is excellent in others belong to us as well. —Voltaire

Sometimes tears are a sign of unspoken happiness and a smile is a sign of silent pain. —Author unknown

No Accounting for Tastes

Words by Liz Stout

ONES always chew more than they have bitten off.

TWOS offer a bite to someone else first.

THREES take a bite of the best-selling, most popular brand.

FOURS take a bite slowly and dramatically, hoping others are watching.

FIVES hide the wrapper so no one else will
know what bites they are enjoying.

SIXES check the expiration date or read the
list of ingredients before taking a bite.

SEVENS *do* bite off more than they
can chew, and proceed to chew it.

EIGHTS may take possession of someone
else's bite, putting up a fight if necessary.

NINES can't make up their minds what to take a bite of;
they take a little of everything so as not to show partiality.

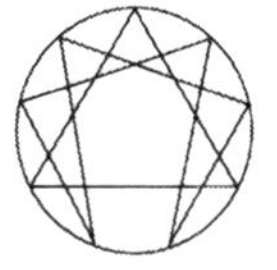

Enneagram Type 3 – The Achiever

You never get a second chance to make a good first impression.
—Head & Shoulders commercial

Part I: Are YOU an Achiever?

Ambience: Charming

Attire: Stylish, the right brand

Good at: Working hard, inspiring others, having lots of Facebook friends

Good with: Mentoring one-to-one, inspiring groups to great heights

Noise level: Normal

Take away: Practical, get-it-done attitude

Influences: Achievers are influenced by their wings on each side of their number, the 2-Helper and the 4-Romantic. They are also influenced by the two types connected by lines, called arrows. The 6-Questioner and the 9-Peace Seeker arrows can be used for growth, for example when the Achiever wants to be more loyal (6) or slow down and relax (9). See the Enneagram diagram in the Preface.

Success is liking yourself, liking what you do, and liking how you do it. – Maya Angelou

Achiever quiz based on statements by adolescents

How many of these ten sentences do you agree with?

Description

☐ I'm competitive, aggressive in getting tasks done, and good at motivating others. I'm a player, not a spectator. —Darryl

☐ I believe first impressions are important. I like to pick good friends who dress nice and make a good impression on me. —Darryl

☐ My friends tell me I am always there when they need a smile. —Darryl

☐ I want to be seen as popular and successful. —Bill

What's the worst thing that can happen to an Achiever?

- [ ] My worst nightmare is having people see me mess up badly or saying something stupid and looking dumb.—Darryl
- [ ] Becoming a dirty homeless person.—Bill

What can you learn?

- [ ] It's true that sometimes I'm shallow and vain. I can work on that. —Bill
- [ ] I could work on learning better how to entertain myself. —Darryl

How do you keep your boundaries?

- [ ] When I'm doing the best I can to get something done and people are saying "can't you hurry it up?" I get mad and I say things like, "look here I am doing the best I can and if you have a problem with it you can leave." —Bill
- [ ] With close family, I became moody and outwardly disparaged anyone that would interact with me. With those I wanted to impress I would shut down my emotions and feel the need to be liked. —Brian

You're an Achiever if you check five or more of these boxes and identify with more cartoons and interviews in this chapter than in the other chapters.

Famous Achievers include: Rachael Berry, Justin Bieber, Tom Cruise, Taylor Swift, Denzel Washington, and Oprah Winfrey.

Part II: Being an Achiever

These go from youngest to oldest—from people who are adolescents now to adults recalling their adolescence.

Darryl the Charmer

I like it when I have won a title or recognition; I also like dressing and try to make a good impression. I'm good at organizing projects and people, communicating, goal setting, and making decisions. I'm proud of success and like to be part of the action. Last but not least, I'm sociable and charming. I also take on traits of other numbers including my wings, which are the 2-Helper and the 4-Romantic and my arrows, the 6-Questioner and the 9-Peace Seeker.

Running for office

When I got elected to be on student counsel, which to tell you the truth I didn't think I was going to get, I was proud of what I accomplished and I liked representing our school. First impressions are important. I'd never want to look like I just got out of bed. It might seem sad but I don't like to hang out with people who are dirty. That is probably a big hint that I'm a 3.

Getting things done

Sometimes I get mad and tell people what I think, like when the student counsel was helping with the Italian sodas at the winter luau and there was a long line. People were saying stuff like "hurry up we don't have all day," and you know they really are worth the wait. So I guess I am pretty aggressive in getting things done and getting things through to people when I talk. I am also a good writer.

Soaring

I can also motivate people when they are feeling down or not feeling wanted. I can make them get from sad to happy in no time at all. When I moved away, my friends told me I was always there when they needed a smile and I could really lift their spirits when they were down or any time.

When I had read all of the things about me I started thinking to myself, oh my gosh that is so me I couldn't believe it. The 3-Achiever is a good thing to be because we are good team players and succeed in almost everything we do. —Darryl

Bill the Competitor

A 3-Achiever is a person who wants to be seen as successful and popular. We are intense and often times are good at sports. I like taking on projects and am always doing something, whether it be playing a sport or cooking. I also like to be in front of people. When I was younger I loved putting models together. It didn't matter if it was a car or an airplane, my brother and I would work for days trying to make our models perfect.

Practicing this way, the Giants were highly motivated not to drop the ball.

Sports

I am especially competitive in sports. That's why my brother doesn't like golfing with me. Football is my favorite sport if you haven't guessed it yet—because of the action and contact.

Vanity

I want to be seen as popular. I mean who doesn't? And successful. I am sometimes vain and can't stand it when people see me mess up badly. After I act a little shallow and vain, sometimes I fall into my worst nightmare by saying something totally stupid. Then I look dumb myself.

I'm not sure how the Enneagram book I read knew all of these things but I'm glad it did because it helped me learn more about myself. —Bill

Highly Motivated Isabella

Personal drive is the key factor. I judge myself by how much I accomplish and always try to do things better than other people. I had two different roommates during my first year at university I had known in high school. Each of these girls was actually smarter and got better grades than

I (one of them tutored me to help me pass my one math class!), but they both dropped out our freshman year to get married. They had only gone to university because their parents had wanted them to. Unlike me, they had no personal motivation to be there. —Isabella

Sensitive Brian

Wanting to fit in was a huge deal to me growing up. I wanted to be liked and accepted by my family and friends. In fact, that someone should think ill of me was extremely terrifying. I did all I could to be all things to all people. Unfortunately, this way of being actually deprived me from what I wanted most, connection and community with my peers.

Need to fit in

My need to be liked made life in middle and high school extremely challenging. My intense desire to be part of the "cool" crowd—the crowd I assessed as having the greatest social value in my school—made me hyper self-conscious about who I was being to fit in. I came across as needy, confused and insecure—all of which were true. I was looking for external validation from the peer group I wanted to be associated with instead of just being me.

Who am I?

The irony lies in the fact that I had no earthly idea as to who I really was. As long as I could remember, I was trying to be what I thought other people wanted me to be—and that would change from person to person or peer group to peer group. So, when I started at a new school at the age of 13, my parents' advice was "just be yourself." I thought to myself, who the heck is that? I still feel sad about how lost I was as a child and adolescent. I never felt I was appreciated for being who I truly was, so I always defaulted to being something else to win the approval of others. I feared "being myself" because of the risk that my real self would not be liked. This created a paradox—I couldn't be me, because someone may not like it, yet I couldn't be who I thought they wanted me to be, because then I would appear "fake."

Sensitive

I was an incredibly sensitive child. I was ashamed of my sensitivity because my father and friends thought that was a sign of weakness—"men aren't supposed to be sensitive in this culture." My peers would make fun of me for that. I felt something was wrong with me—if men aren't supposed to be sensitive, why am I so damn sensitive?! I better hide it so that I can appear normal and fit in. This taught me to cut off myself from my emotions and to strategically display parts of myself I deemed were "acceptable" in the moment. I also cut myself off from truly connecting with others, which only further amplified my loneliness and shame.

Boundaries

When I felt my boundaries were threatened I would shift my being dramatically in two different ways:

With loved ones I cared for and trusted: nice/gentle/caring Brian would turn into wrathful "don't f--- with me Brian." I'd become moody and disparage anyone that would interact with me. I would project my own inner feelings of worthlessness out onto them. If anyone were to cross my path, I would make sure they felt as crappy and as worthless as I did. My mom learned early on she would need to give me space when I was in this place as I was unreceptive to anything the outside world had to say.

With those I didn't know as well or wanted to impress: when my boundaries were threatened, I would shut down my emotions and resort to my inner sanctum. I would be "in my head," trying to appear normal to outside viewers.

My need for being liked would become much stronger and I would become needy. Needing to be liked/wanted would backfire as I became unpleasant to be around. I was trying harder and harder, as if the volume knob on my "self-conscious meter" would be turned up to 10. —Brian

Don and His Dads

I found my father dead when I was 13 and a half. When I got home from school at 3:45, my dad was asleep in his bed. I went to the park to play basketball. Two hours later some police arrived to take me home. Relatives had already gathered—my mother belonged to a close-knit Scottish clan. The police knew my father as a drunk they would escort home from the bar. As we entered the walkway to my house, one of them said, "Your dad's passed away. Say your prayers."

Abusive father

I was in shock. I didn't like the emotion I was having—of deep relief. Ages 10 – 13 had been the worst—a blur of beatings. My father thought spankings were demeaning so he inflicted disciplinary boxing matches on me. He was incredibly strong, the Pacific Fleet Boxing Champion during World War II. I was small for my age. Dad was a mechanic, butcher, and singer in a nightclub. He was from a strict Norwegian Lutheran family and had been beaten himself. It was against the religion to drink. He ran away from his own family and tried to make me a warrior and give me family discipline.

I will prevail

The bully

The second day of 7th grade, the biggest neighborhood bully, an Armenian kid three years older than me, targeted me on the bus and threw my books out the window. I told my dad and immediately got another boxing match. He pummeled me and insisted I go on an honor quest to get the $42.00 back for my lost textbooks. Kids in my neighborhood rejected the Armenian kid. He was big, hairy, and frightening. I had altogether seven fights with him. If I didn't show he had bruised me, my dad would beat me himself.

I *got* the bully by mistake. When I climbed up on a neighbor's roof to retrieve a basketball, his head popped up and I kicked him in the face. He fell backwards six feet down. I jumped on him and pinned his arms with my knees. Then I pummeled him. He was a bloody wreck and didn't go to school for two weeks. His mom came from across the street and hit me with a broom. I hit her back with it.

My dad and I went to the kid's front door and asked his dad for the $42.00. He gave us cash. I had hero status for the rest of junior high school and into high school.

Also, things improved between me and my dad, including going fishing.

One good thing about my dad was that he insisted on reading to me and had me read the world's classics. I was always good in school—the teacher's pet. I had wonderful teachers. People paid attention to me.

Music

I played violin from ages 6 to 14, but I associated it with my father, "he who must be obeyed," and quit after he died. The relief and guilt about my father stay with me to this day. Later I studied the Spanish guitar tradition, which contributed to my social life in a major way. I had a repertoire of about 60 songs. At 15 I started a folk music club. I became an impresario and brought folk acts to my high school at lunchtime from The Ash Grove in Los Angeles, the center of a vibrant folk-rock scene. This made me popular in my high school of 5,000.

Athletic

I was a good athlete. I pitched baseball and played football—good at blocking and catching. I used my violent side. I was also on the golf team and swim team.

Playing the crowd

Threes can change roles and status and can become the other person. My greatest ability and greatest character flaw is that I understand other people and play to the audience. I become what people want me to be because I can. My greatest act of maturity was when I quit doing that, but it was after my adolescence.

I became a diplomat. The Cultural Exchange Representative with the United States Information Service chose me out of 150 students to go to 18 countries for two weeks. Then I ended up in Nepal. I was an advanced speaker on almost every topic, a huckster, a gifted storyteller, and a persuader. I lectured on American culture and politics and I propounded women's rights and nonviolence. I knew United States history well because my mother taught it. After I exposed the American Empire, they ended this program. I was the single cause—the State Department received complaints about me.

Romance

I had my first big romance at age 11. I fell in love with Cindy in 5th grade. I was awkward, unskilled, and tried to court her, but she rejected the boxes of spiders and toads I put on her desk. I carried this scar of rejection my whole life. We Threes have a fear of rejection.

Stepfather didn't like me

My mother remarried—a man who was a homebody and a college professor—a blazing 5-Observer. He liked to cook, spoke nine languages, had a photographic memory, and a PhD in philology from Harvard. He didn't like me. Achievers resist being known intimately and Observers want the truth and reality. I insisted on the mythic-poetic. I was gooey and he was dry. He was always trying to expose me as a fraud.

Nature mystic

At age 16 I worked in construction and spent the summer high on peyote one of the other workers had brought. I became an eccentric artistic outrider in Topanga Canyon in Los Angeles, an artist colony. At 15 I studied Zen Buddhism, the most nonviolent religion, to overcome the violence in my life. I was a peace and love hippie and a vegetarian.

I considered myself a nature mystic (the connection to my 9-Peace Seeker arrow). The profound unified experience of the visible and invisible was the most important experience in my life. I fell into the pathway of friendly sex as opposed to chasing girls. I liked extending out to another person as a friend. I lost the fear of being found out or known, and I didn't feel as bound. I wasn't worried about my image. I was freer.

At 17, at a time when all my friends had long hair, I cut my hair. My Scottish grandfather died and I wore his clothes—golf shirts and pants and white shoes. I looked really different and didn't care what people thought.

Paris

My stepfather sent me to study French in Paris at age 17 for three and a half months. I didn't want to go. I wanted to stay home and body surf. But my stepfather didn't want me around. I was exposed to a lot of things I was not, which helped me become more authentic. I knew I was a 20th century American. I met a tall, elegant black woman in my class. Beullah was from a well-educated, stable Jamaican family. She was about 18, a model, and had never had a boyfriend. We studied French literature, went to African parties, and spent two hours a day at the Louvre. I fit in and became an international citizen.

Sometimes things happen against your will that are good for you. This goes against the "3's need to push people around." 3's are like the = sign in the equation, balancing two opposites. We're good at negotiating. My best compliment was when I was ten years old. My grandfather said, "I noticed you can learn from others' mistakes. It's unusual." There are two sides to this: I can see things from other points of view but this allows me to manipulate them. —Don

Charlotte, Just Tolerated

I was an only child with no Daddy. Mother worked as a billing clerk. Grandma, whose house we lived in, just tolerated me, and no one expected anything from me. As far back as first grade I wanted to show off. I had movie star photos pinned all over the beaverboard walls on the enclosed back porch where Mother and I slept in an old double bed with a sagging Beautyrest mattress. If I saw something I could win or be good at, I went for it, like having perfect Sunday school attendance—because if you got a pin or a ribbon, it meant you're somebody and that's a lot better than being nobody. In ninth grade, classmates applauded my girl friend, Sandra, and me for harmonizing a popular song. I got excited thinking this could go somewhere! I begged Mother for some money to buy just one piece of sheet music, and talked another girl friend into being our accompanist. I was already picturing us wearing long fur coats, dangling rhinestone earrings and big smiles and I could see my name in lights.

Competing

In the meantime, I taught myself to play tennis by hitting balls off the side of the house all afternoon. Our P.E. teacher teamed me up with another girl, Patsy, and we won our first city tournament. We won silver cups. The more I did the more pressure I felt because staying popular meant always doing something else to impress people. I didn't want to lose. Ever. Listen, the day I graduated from high school and the principal handed me my diploma, he leaned in and asked if we'd won the state tournament that morning, I had to say, "We lost." That's all I ever think about when I think about high school graduation, even though I'd been awarded a freshman scholarship to the State University. —Charlotte

Part III: The Achiever and the Seven Goals

1. **Developing the habits of accomplishing daily tasks and studying effectively** (see #5). Achievers usually excel at working hard.

2. **Being mindful of your body.** Achievers usually excel at this too, because they want to make a good impression and stay active. When they overdo it, however, their sleep and health suffer.

3. **Being mindful of how you treat your friends, your parents, your siblings, your community, and your teachers**. You are probably an extravert and like having lots of friends, though some Achievers are introverts.

4. **Being mindful of your emotional/spiritual development.** This can be a challenge to you if you're overly focused on what other people think of you instead of your own feelings. The Enneagram is useful by pointing out areas you may want to work on, in this case your inner life.

5. **Nurturing your intellect.** This is one of the most important ways to prepare you for the future.

Your Learning Style

- You probably control your environment, are decisive, and focus on structure.
- When you study, you will be happiest if you link up with a broad range of people, unless you are a less common introverted Achiever.
- Be careful not to sign up for so many activities that you become overly stressed.

6. **Develop interests based on your passions and values.** Sometimes Achievers have difficulty knowing what they like as opposed to what others expect them to like. Rate what feels the most rewarding when you go places, read, and study. Develop your own interests.

7. **Educate yourself on career choices** that incorporate your innate strengths of being able to read and inspire people, the drive to win, being efficient, the ability to work hard, and the ability to take risks.

   What interests you—business, construction, manufacturing, education, healthcare, education, information technology, literature, arts, entertainment, math, engineering, science, the human potential movement, the law, the military, or something else? Whatever it is, you will enjoy climbing the ladder of success in the company you work for.

Part IV: What I like about being an Achiever

Part V: Healing Words for Achievers

Never mind what others do; do better than yourself, beat your own record from day to day, and you are a success. —William J. H. Boetcker

If you come in second, you're just the first loser! —Tiger Woods

The fruits of life fall into the hands of those who climb the tree and pick them. —Earl Tupper

It's healthy to spend time alone. You need to know how to spend time alone and not be defined by another person. —Oscar Wilde

Do the right thing, even when no one is looking. —Anonymous

The Enneagram of Statuary
3
7
TWO
VIII
FIVE
SIX
FOUR
Nine

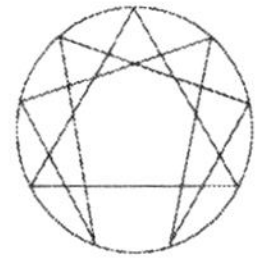

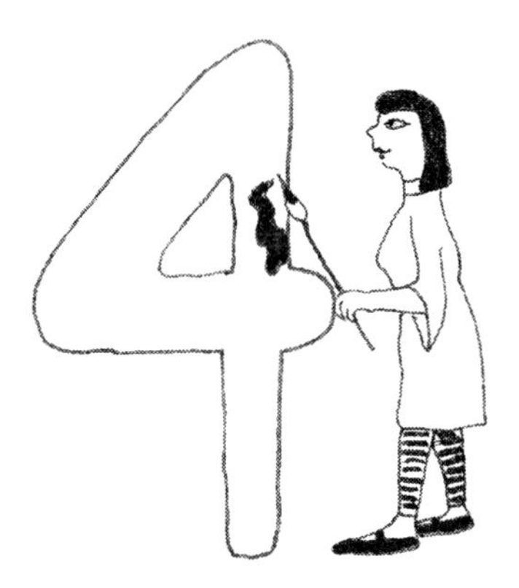

Enneagram Type 4 – The Romantic

There is something pleasurable in calm remembrance of a past sorrow.
—Cicero

Part I: Are YOU a Romantic?

Ambience: The unbearable angst of being an emo

Attire: Could be gothic or artistic

Good at: Being compassionate and noticing what's special about people and things

Good with: Artistic types, other goths

Noise level: Often a soft, buttery voice

Take away: Distinctive, unusual, even unique

Influences: Romantics are influenced by their wings on each side of their number, the 3-Achiever and the 5-Observer. They are also influenced by the two types connected by lines, called arrows. The 1-Perfectionist and the 2-Helper arrows can be used for growth, for example when the Romantic wants to be better organized (1) or more involved with people (2). See the Enneagram diagram in the Preface.

Romantic quiz based on statements by adolescents

How many of these ten sentences do you agree with?

Description

☐ I want to be unique, to be understood, to find meaning to life, and to be seen as special. —Mei Xing

☐ I admit I do not have the sunniest overview of life. —Chiara

☐ Whether I'm depressed or happy, I love to unload my emotions. —Chiara

☐ I like to be noticed but I'd rather be nothing than try too hard to be known and make a fool out of myself in the process. —Chiara

What's the worst thing that can happen to a Romantic?

☐ Even the slightest crude remark can hurt me deeply. —Chiara

☐ For people to think I'm weird because I'm different. —Mei Xing

What can you learn?

☐ I don't know if I need to change this, but some people don't like it that I cry and get too excited over the littlest things. – Kaitlin

☐ I'm emotionally intense. I'd like to learn how to voice my opinions without feeling like everyone is looking at me funny. —Shuan

How do you keep your boundaries?

I dress like I'm a piece of art and if people don't like the way I look they stay away from me. —Hunter

A way to not worry about boundaries is to stay by myself a lot and make friends with books, nature, and my own private symbols, like flowers and art.—Chiara

You're a Romantic if you checked five or more of these and identify with more cartoons and interviews in this chapter than in the other chapters.

Beauty, dignity, mystery

Famous Romantics include: Lana Del Rey, Johnny Depp, Selena Gomez,

Ariana Grande, Michael Jackson, Angelina Jolie, and Ed Sheeran.

Part II: Being a Romantic

These go from youngest to oldest—from adolescents now to adults recalling their adolescence.

Drawing from "The Enneagram of Parenting" by E. Wagele. HarperCollins

Chiara: Symbols and Arts

If I had to pick a personality that suited me best, it would be the 4-Romantic. I don't like having limits on me.

I love symbols, though they must be the right kind—not the pretty-face kind with flowers and hearts flying through the air and peace scribbled all over them. Those make me want to gag. No, I prefer the ones that have feeling, that possess an air of dignity, beauty, and elegance, yet seem kind, wise and a little humorous.

I have a sticker I love of a neat looking frog holding the world in his lap with a peace sign spread across its surface. I like peace, I just like it to be put in a *different* way, like a dove holding an olive branch. Seeing a bunch of peace signs covering a piece of paper seems a bit tacky and timeworn to me. But the frog appeals to me, to the point where I feel like smiling after I look at it.

Love of arts

I love many kinds of art—singing and making music, which I do often and am considered fairly good at, and painting, pastel coloring, and charcoal. This is a way for me to unload feelings. Being complimented for my work boosts my self-esteem, making it a fun challenge.

Writing is my favorite art. It makes me feel free and happy, like a breath of fresh air from a window when you have been cooped up in a stuffy house. When I'm writing, I can make any world any way I want. I could make horses have wings and you can fly on their backs. There's no limit. It is the best way for me to unload emotions. I feel rewarded when I please people with what I love to do the most. I like small amounts of helpful criticism as well.

I'm the happiest when I get praise from my mother. I trust her opinion and she doesn't just tell me the good things I did, although she usually does a good job of commending me. The downside to my happiness from writing is that I'm vulnerable to remarks people make. My self-esteem can plummet into a dark pit of sadness.

I like being noticed. When I am in a play, I shoot for a character that has a significant part. I do not care for the feeling of being nothing to nobody. Although I'd rather be that than try too hard to be known and make a fool out of myself in the process. I cannot stand to lose my dignity. But the feeling of uniqueness is one of my favorites, so I like to prove that I am me, a single personality out of billions that cannot be categorized or limited to any great extent. —Chiara

Sensitive and Emotional Kaitlin

Unique, Romantic? I guess that would be me. 4's are the artistic, creative and emotional kind. When I grow up I'd like to have a job as fashion designer, actress, or artist. When I was a little girl all I wanted was dress up clothes and an artist set. My favorite hobby was dressing Barbies up, fixing their hair, and then putting them in plays. I would get so dramatic I would start to cry.

Drama

Ever since then I have put much drama into every little thing I've done. I love fantasy movies, books, and figures. I am so, so sensitive and emotional! I cry and get too excited over the littlest things. For example, when I was in sixth grade when I found out what one of my birthday presents was I started bawling. I loved the present—it was just that I felt so sad.

Nobody's as sad as I am...

Sometimes I feel out of place. Sometimes I think I was a princess mistakenly born into a family of peasants. I'm glad I'm the number 4. I think the Enneagram is interesting and I would like to learn more. It is a good idea to learn about yourself and to say, hey that is like me. —Kaitlin

Mei Xing Cries a Lot

I want to be unique, to be understood, to find meaning to life, and I long for emotional connections with people. Romantics want to be seen as special. They're happy and the next thing you know they're crying. I'm either super happy or I'm bummed. I like Tarot cards, Dracula books, astrology, and Edgar Allen Poe. I cover up my depression when I'm with friends.

Physical image

I'm quiet and mature but I want people to notice me. I get attention by my appearance. Life would be so boring without 4's. People worry about me because I like the color black. If my parents would let me, I'd pierce my eyebrows and belly button and dye my hair a different color every day. I wouldn't care what people thought of me.

I'm so emotional, I cry all the time. When I see a sad movie I cry. When I'm depressed I'm just awful. Everybody knows it when I am having a bad day. That's how I know I am a 4. —Mei Xing

Shuan the Misunderstood

I have the Romantic characteristics of fantasizing and having a good imagination. I'm emotionally sensitive, intense, and feel misunderstood. I am self-critical and feel melancholy or depressed a lot of the time. I was always told I had these characteristics even before I knew anything about the Enneagram.

Depression

Depression is one word I am very familiar with. When I was younger everyone would tell me I was full of hate and always depressed. I went to the doctor and he told me I suffered from depression. I now take an antidepressant called Paxil.

Feeling different

Throughout my life I have felt misunderstood. When people would tell me to be myself, I never felt I could because I always felt different. You feel all alone when you're a 4. Whenever I had an opinion I would voice it, yet I would feel like everyone would look at me funny.

I have always been the type of person who wants to talk everything out. I am emotionally intense and I get stressed out. —Shuan

Drawing from "The Career Within You" by Wagele/Stabb. HarperCollins

Hunter the Poet

I am poetic, searching, longing, dark, deep, unknown, a Romantic. We are soul searching, lovemaking, writing hands and depression-stretched souls, an endless pit fallen through, open eyes and more scenery than one could imagine! Our eyes can feel the hurt of the world and our hands can see its tears. We see not a wretch but a lost soul seeking for refuge and truth that will die a wondering man.

Nothing can be as is. There is always something more.

I see not a weed but an expert on the world around me, a misunderstood beauty that knows that place so well I could paint a picture of it even when capped in night. I know every blade of grass by name, every reed by its unique note when played by the wind. I see a flower that if never there, an insect would have drowned, a butterfly would be more exhausted from having to fly farther to find somewhere to land, possibly too far for its own body to handle, a blank spot in a constant pink and green. If something else had blossomed or grown, where do you think that butterfly would be today? What do you think the scenery would look like now?

Ever since the age of five and six I have been writing poetry. Ever since 6th grade I have taken it seriously. Ever since the middle of 7th grade it has become me. I ponder thoughts others would never dare think. I solve dilemmas in ways any other man would ponder for days.

We 4's go places and create places others couldn't dream of. Our hands create works that paint a picture so vivid you could actually be there.

Our minds are greater than the greatest mountains, our souls are deeper than the deepest chasm, and our minds flow constantly like the oceans with ideas farther than the stars.

We 4's don't have to reach the stars. All we have to do is turn around and look back. —Hunter

Joyce's Two Cultures

I was always searching for something during my teenage years, but what it was I would not find out till years later. In a vague, hazy sort of way, I wanted to know and to be known, to feel connected in this world. But I wouldn't understand what this feeling was until I had to transport myself to and from home for college. There is something about BART (Bay Area Rapid Transit) rides that makes me love commuting from my home in San Jose to Berkeley, where I go to college.

A peaceful feeling

On those 50-minute rides, I feel something rare, something truly special. It's not love; and it's not quite a sense of community. Perhaps it's what Marina Keegan, the student at Yale University who died last year in a car accident, had called "the opposite of loneliness,"[1] an emotion we don't really have a word for in the English language. This feeling is peaceful and unassuming. Sometimes it's more comforting than friends. This was the feeling I had searched for all of my adolescent years.

Lonely

I am Chinese-American, a second-generation immigrant, born to parents from Taiwan, who were born to parents from China. Most of my teenage years were centered around reconciling these two parts of my identity, the Chinese and the American, and trying to figure out where my love for literature and for writing fit into all of it. At school, I satisfy the typical Chinese student stereotypes: I did well in math, was an all-around "A" student, and took Chinese school over the weekends. That came from my Chinese side, from the values my parents instilled in me. And yet, the discourse I used to interact with my teachers and peers—from the way I talked and dressed to the way I thought—that came from my American side, my American environment. What side did my love for the books that opened worlds of wonder for me and the images their language created belong to? It wasn't really encouraged by either. As you may guess, this made it hard to belong in any of the groups of people in my life at the time, and although I was never at a lack of friends to hang out with and was always surrounded by people, I was gnawingly lonely.

University

It wasn't until I was given the opportunity to explore and allowed to be a little left of center at the University of California (Cal) in Berkeley that I found a way to reconcile these different aspects of myself. I am now a Comparative Literature major with an Education minor. As a Comparative Literature major, my major language is English and my minor language is Chinese. In this way, I am able to study literature from both of my cultural backgrounds. In this way, I am also able to find "the opposite of loneliness" as another Humanities major in a sea of Cal students. —Joyce

---

[1] Keegan, Marina. "The Opposite of Loneliness." http://yaledailynews.com/crosscampus/2012/05/27/keegan-the-opposite-of-loneliness/.

Delia's Inner Life

I spent a lot of my early adolescence wandering the hills alone with my dog singing pop tunes, reading books, or writing poems. I had mystery places in the hills. I put flowers as an offering, to what I don't know, in still, quiet places in the creek and in a mound of rocks. I had one best friend and a couple of others. I was very spiritual. At ten I had the sense I was destined for something grand and special. I also wanted to be a famous singer. One morning I decided I was never going to do a bad thing, but by the afternoon I had not kept my promise.

My first major trauma was when my dog died. I was depressed for weeks.

Clothes

In Jr. High I was one of the less popular kids. I didn't dress well and resented the idea of conforming and being in style. Mom wouldn't spend much money on clothes but it was also a case of misplaced idealism. At 14 or 15 I gave in, started dressing better, and felt less stressed. I wish I had discovered thrift shops and had gone looking for my own clothes. I could have been more enterprising. I was always waiting until I grew up.

At 12 I asked for piano lessons but I didn't like the teacher. I wish I had taken charge. I would have asked to learn how to improvise and play pop instead of classical and I would have earned more money for lessons.

Bullying

Kids were mean. I was skinny and boys would call me a dog, meaning an ugly girl, or a can opener because of my buckteeth. They'd go woof, woof when I walked by. Bullies followed me, often in groups, and threatened me and hit me sometimes. I didn't have good social skills. I was smarter than average and I'd imply the bullies were insecure. One bully was a girl. I wasn't a lesbian but she'd yell, "Hey little lesbian, when you gonna kiss me?"

Taking the bull by the horns.

When I was 13 we moved from a suburban area to a bedroom community where there was no open land and I could no longer be alone in nature. Kids were very style-conscious there. A big breakthrough was that I found a soulmate, a hippie-ish girl I liked a lot. At 15 and a half I had my first boyfriend.

Nature, music, friends, my dog, and books were a huge comfort to me in my adolescence. —Delia

Anne's Lonely Adolescence

My childhood was relatively happy, but when I hit adolescence I was unable to ignore issues that had developed earlier but had stayed underground. In other words, the shit hit the fan.

Changing schools

At the beginning of seventh grade, I changed schools because we moved to a more prosperous area of the city, supposedly for the benefit of my younger sister and me. Unfortunately, it was the beginning of a very difficult time, which lasted all the way through high school.

I had felt comfortable in the working class neighborhood where I lived for my first eleven years, but I never felt I fit in with the cliquish rich kids in my new school. They had known each other for years and did not welcome new people. Unfortunately, my parents could not help me integrate into this new social scene. Instead my mother made me wrong for not having the friends she thought I should have. She was generally critical towards me, comparing me to other girls who were more popular. (Now I understand that she herself felt insecure in this new neighborhood and also didn't have friends when she was in school, but at the time it was painful to be rejected by both her and my peers.)

Isolated

So I felt alone and isolated, with no one to talk to about my experience. I longed for authentic connections with people—openness, honesty, and truth, rather than the falseness, superficiality and closed-heartedness I saw around me. And I thought it was my fault, that there was something wrong with me, some basic flaw that kept me from being accepted, loved, and appreciated.

Fortunately, I found ways to avoid feeling bad all the time, to connect with who I really was beneath the exterior of a shy girl who didn't fit in. I found consolation in academics, music, books, and with a neighbor who was a role model.

I was always a good student and got from my teachers the positive feedback I didn't get at home. My goal in high school was to get good grades and go to a college far away from the limited, rejecting atmosphere I felt trapped in (I succeeded at this, winning a scholarship from a prestigious women's college.)

Singing

Listening to music and singing in the school chorus with an inspiring conductor were ways to connect with and express a deeper part of myself. I felt real and alive when I sang. I knew this was what I should be doing and more important than the social life I didn't have. (I am now a professional classical singer.)

Reading

I also found solace in literature, finding evidence in novels and biographies that there could be travel, art, and intellectual and spiritual pursuits—more to life than the mundane existences I saw around me.

Role model

I was fortunate enough to have living proof of this in the form of a neighbor—an older European-born woman who was living in the attic apartment of our house with her invalid husband and had previously lived in exotic places like Shanghai and Cairo. She was a writer and classical music lover, a traveler, a free spirit—the kind of person I wanted to be (and have become). We listened to music together and talked about books; my time with her was special and precious. I was able express to her a little of the frustration I felt living in a world I didn't feel part of—but not too much because I felt my inability to fit in was due to some basic deficiency in me, and I was ashamed for her to see that.

So my adolescence was not a happy time (is anybody's?), but I survived it by moving towards the activities and people I felt authentically connected with and away from those that felt negative, in the hope that I would eventually find love and acceptance from people I wanted to be with—which I have! —Anne

Bob's Interests—Law and Writing

My father was a lawyer and my mother a schoolteacher-turned housewife. I was a first child, the center of attention, and early on had the idea I was meant for special things. When my sister and brother came along, I resented the competition but never lost my sense of specialness.

When I was ten, my sister died. It threw my parents into a depression and turned our house into an unhappy place. Without knowing that's what I was doing, I started building a life outside it.

Private school

This life had two prongs. The first was at the private school my parents had transferred me to from our local public one. It had a suburban, WASP, elitist culture, which I tried to fit into by playing sports and engaging in extra curricular activities and getting good grades without working too hard. I was pretty successful at making the "in" crowd, though, being Jewish, I was never going to totally fit. In my neighborhood, which was mostly Jewish, middle- and lower-middle class, I was less successful, since I was this "private school kid," and there most of my friends were outsiders, and we were into things like banned comics, rhythm and blues, and later, jazz. I thought I was just moving smoothly along, but really I was making choices, picking up pieces both places of who I was to become.

College

I went to a small, progressive liberal arts college. I thought I was going to be a lawyer like my father. But the college was all about grades, and mine were not too good. How could I be a special lawyer, I thought, with a C+/B- average?

The only thing I was good at was writing. There I got A's. This was shocking. I wasn't part of the campus literary crowd. My parents didn't know a writer or artist or musician. But I liked the idea. The college culture extolled individualism and non-conformity, and writing promised that. My parents, meanwhile, were appalled.

So I took the law boards—and did well. Now I had evidence I could be a good lawyer. Plus, I needed a draft deferment, and writing wouldn't get me one of those. I was accepted at law school and enrolled and was there when the full force of the '60s hit. It was all working on me: fate and genes, history and psycho-dynamics, and choice. —Bob

Part III: The Romantic and the Seven Goals

1. **Developing the habit of using your time wisely for studying and chores** (see #5). Your Perfectionist arrow and Achiever wing are good models for this.

2. **Being mindful of your body.** As a Romantic you probably already pay a lot of attention to how you look. Romantics often dress with an artistic flair, which is easy to spot.

3. **Being mindful of your relationship to your friends, your parents, your siblings, your community, and your teachers**. As a Romantic, you are likely to be introverted and have a few meaningful friends as opposed to many casual acquaintances.

4. **Being mindful of your emotional/spiritual development** is probably easy for you if you are a soul-searcher or poet by nature.

Healthy Romantics are capable of a depth of feeling most of us have no access to. They are better than most others at understanding and guiding people in psychic distress. They are not intimidated by the difficult, complicated, or dark feelings of others since they themselves have lived through it all. - From The Enneagram—a Christian Perspective by Richard Rohr and Andreas Ebert.

If you want others to be happy, practice compassion. If you want to be happy, practice compassion. —Dalai Lama

5. **Nurture your intellect, logical thinking, problem solving, and ability to acquire knowledge.** Access your 1-Perfectionist arrow or your 5-Observer wing for discipline when working on this goal.

Your Learning Style

- Most Romantics are introverted and sensitive. You probably like a personalized, feeling approach to learning and prefer small groups. Sometimes you prefer *not* being noticed in a large impersonal classroom, where you can take time to digest what you have learned.
- Be careful not to take criticism or feedback personally.

- You probably don't like being put on the spot and need time to process new information. If these are problems, discuss them with your teacher.
- Make use of your ability to express yourself in an unusual, creative way.
- You are likely to be interested in diversity, possibilities for people, human growth and development, and/or the arts.

6. **Develop interests based on your passions and values.** If you are an introverted Romantic, especially, you are already likely to be interested in your values and what is important to you.

7. **Educate yourself on career choices that incorporate your innate strengths**, including valuing what is authentic, being compassionate, the gift for interpreting meaning from one person to another, being creative, and being dauntless. What interests you—literature, arts, entertainment, education, healthcare, the human potential movement, business, construction, manufacturing, information technology, math, engineering, science, the law, or something else? Whatever it is, you are sure to add your perception and compassion to the workplace.

Part IV: What I Like about being a Romantic

Part V: Healing Words for a Romantic

The invariable mark of wisdom is to see the miraculous in the common.
—Ralph Waldo Emerson

Be yourself. An original is always worth more than a copy.
—Author unknown

School spirit is something everyone wants but few are willing to take the risk to express in a unique way. —Author unknown

Elegance is when the inside is as beautiful as the outside. —Coco Chanel

Romantics find beauty in things others don't even notice.
—Author unknown

It's okay to not be okay. —Author unknown

The Enneagram of Dogs
1
I TOLD you not to do it on the rug!
Whippet?
2
You-are-so-beautiful to-o me
Joe Cocker Spaniel
3
POP
I'm on my way to the top!
Welsh Corki
4
Virginia Woof
5
Shepnerd
6
AM I STILL CUTE?
7
Lets have a picnic!
Basket Hound
8
Doberman Pinscher
9
zzzzzz
Schnoozer

Enneagram Type 5 – The Observer

You can observe a lot just by watching. —Yogi Berra

Part I: Are YOU an Observer?

Ambience: Gentle, whimsical sense of humor

Attire: Often casual

Good at: Gathering knowledge, logic, ordering information

Good with: Computers, things that take dedicated concentration

Noise level: Quiet

Take away: Objectivity and the desire to learn

Influences: Observers are influenced by their wings on each side of their number, the 4-Romantic and 6-Questioner. They are also influenced by the two types connected by lines, called arrows. The 7-Adventurer and 8-Asserter arrows can be used for growth, for example when the Observer wants to be more playful (7) or decisive (8). See the Enneagram diagram in the Preface.

Observer quiz based on statements by adolescents

How many of these ten sentences do you agree with?

Description

- ☐ I like to have knowledge about what I'm doing; I'm curious about everything. —Bradley
- ☐ I like to see things clearly. —Terrell
- ☐ I can go a long time without talking to or seeing another person. —Terrell
- ☐ I tend to avoid social situations and I lack intrapersonal skills. —Brett

What's the worst thing that can happen to an Observer?

- ☐ When people think I'm unhappy because I'm not an extravert and they try to change me. —Terrell

- ☐ When people are noisy or intrude on me when I'm trying to concentrate. —Brett

What can you learn?

- ☐ I feel insecure, almost threatened, when in a crowd and I hate having to give speeches in class. I could learn to not fear these things so much. —Bradley
- ☐ I can try to remember I don't really have to be the one person in the class who knows more than anybody else. —Terrell

How do you keep your boundaries?

- ☐ Instead of sitting with my group of friends, I sit by myself and am my own best friend and still have just as much fun. —Logan
- ☐ One way I keep boundaries is to be always sitting behind the crowd and observing what everyone else is doing. I also get angry at people who barge in on me when I'm on my computer. —Terrell

You're an Observer if you check five or more of these boxes and identify with more cartoons and interviews in this chapter than in the other chapters.

Famous Observers include: The Buddha, David Byrne, Bill Gates, Daniel Day Lewis, Michelle Pfeiffer, and Mark Zuckerberg.

Part II: Being an Observer

Watching

These go from youngest to oldest—from adolescents to adults recalling their adolescence.

Logan the Loner

The 5-Observer personality is based on fear. We're afraid of the world announcing that we are completely wrong. So to stay away from the hard-hitting world, we draw into ourselves and are usually uncomfortable in social situations. Instead of sitting down with our group of friends, we sit by ourselves and are our own best friend and still have just as much fun.

Observers want to know everything. We have to in order to be always right. If we are not right, we fear the world will rush in and say we are wrong. To know everything, we 5's develop masterful observation skills. While not appearing to pay attention, in reality we are and are taking stock of the rest of the room as well (or if we have selective observation, just the room). To be right in school, having a sense of logic helps. This is also a common ability in 5's.

My biggest fear used to be being wrong and I used to get all upset when I was. I don't care if my friends are with me or not because I can do just as well without them. I also appear to know everything. My sense of logic really helps in math. All these abilities point to a 5, so that's what I am. —Logan

I'm not good at expressing my feelings, so I keep everything bottled inside. Half the time, I want to tell someone what I'm feeling, but I don't even know how to describe it...so I stay quiet. —Author unknown

Bradley the Student

Observers, thinkers, always want to know more. We like to amaze people with our knowledge. We are masters of the mind, the wise men who live all alone. We stand in a tower watching the world around us grow. Before we do anything, we always study it. We are curious about everything. If there is something sitting in front of us we do not know much of, we will study, ponder, and determine what it is in our mind.

We like to sit in the back, observing the class around us. Sometimes we seem like we are just daydreaming, but we are listening to everything, trying to constantly learn. We also can easily entertain ourselves watching TV, playing on a computer, reading, or simply thinking. I don't like to talk a lot and it bothers me when other people do. We don't like to get in social things too much. We do not like being the most noticed person, preferring not to be seen much at all.

Hiding

Embarrassment

I hate to be embarrassed and I am embarrassed easily. I love to learn of new things in school, but hate having to give speeches and such. When I am at home, I prefer to be by myself playing at my computer. I could sit and play on it for hours, and even do all my work on it, like writing this document. If there is one thing I hate about society it's all its big crowds. I feel insecure, almost threatened, when in a crowd.

Drawing from "The Career Within You" by Wagele / Stabb. HarperCollins

5's are coming into their own here with new technology advances like the Internet and computer games and the many, many, many books out there to read. I could spend hours and hours just reading books or topics on the Internet, as long as I am alone and away from my little sister! —Bradley

Don't trust atoms. They make up everything. —Author unknown

Terrell Likes Math

We Observers like to see things clearly. We can go a long time without talking or seeing another person. We are always observing what everyone else is doing. 5's are the computer people of the world. If it were not for 5's, the best computer anyone would have would be a 66 MHz with 4 MB of RAM and 200 MB hard drive.

I know I am a 5 because I can sit on my butt in front of a computer screen in a dark room and play a really fun game for a day straight. Sometimes I find myself sitting in the back of the room, observing people. The last thing is that I am really good at math but I suck super bad at art stuff. —Terrell

Quiet Brett

We are generally quiet people who have a tendency to just watch what is happening around us. We see what is going on remarkably well. We are happy when alone and are able to entertain ourselves or sit in front of a computer screen for long periods of time. We are generally thinkers and revel in knowledge and having the most of it.

5's tend to avoid social situations and may lack intrapersonal skills. We are not interested in confrontation and are often emotionally detached from the situation. We are often seen as strange because we do not readily involve ourselves in social groups. Instead, we feel included when we watch. We may become lost in fantastic worlds and often drift off the subject while thinking about something else.

Sometimes I read during class and get so engrossed that I even tune out the lunch bell! Once I learned about the Enneagram and my type, I began to see more about my personality I never noticed before. I like to become knowledgeable about my interests, and I like to learn the nitty-gritty facts, numbers, and terminology so I can correct people. I guess I just revel in my personality type. It's just the way I want to be! —Brett

Elizabeth the Poor

I grew up in a small housing project. My father suffered from alcoholism. Our neighborhood was incredibly dangerous and violent. In order to get out of the projects our family moved into a partially condemned apartment building that had no running hot water, faulty electricity and 'furry guests' :). The toughest years for our family came during my parents' divorce. I was in 7th grade at the time and we lived briefly with my mother's parents, then moved into a low-income duplex. Food and clothing were a constant challenge. I would be sent to the nurse's office and unable to attend class because I wasn't properly dressed.

Sharing with siblings

I constantly worried about my siblings who attended a separate elementary school because I knew they hadn't eaten the night before. I started babysitting at a young age and used my income to buy them food.

I went through a growth spurt and none of my clothes fit and often there was no food in the house, as in none. I used to take my babysitting money and buy a sub sandwich and cut it in three pieces to feed my siblings and myself.

Bullying

I knew how hard my mother was working to put our life back together but that didn't stop kids at school from bullying me. When you are uncomfortable in your own body its a huge distraction. I remember feeling hungry at lunch and having to make random excuses every day for why I wasn't eating (and why we weren't on the roster for free lunch) and why I wore my mother's clothes or the same clothes that didn't fit everyday (I was all legs and arms and nose with pimples. Oh the humility of puberty! Haha.) We also changed school systems four times in three years, moving from our apartment with my father to our grandparents', to our own place, then to a new place with my mother's new boyfriend, and a year after that to an island.

There wasn't time to stop and feel sorry for ourselves and the one constant my mother kept in our lives was a faith education. I would fantasize about someday having a home with matching furniture, a closet full of nice clothes, and good food in the kitchen, similar to what my mother's parents had.

My mother's poverty was a choice because she left her middle class home when she was 17. I would sometimes remind her, when she romanticized our life (that somehow being poor was noble), that my poverty had not been a choice. —Elizabeth

Jaki's Irrational Mother

From 10-14 I was in the process of learning my mother wasn't always right, and was, in fact, irrational at times. I asked a friend's mother if she was really a spy as my mother had told me. She said no. I started to question the irrational side of my mother's words, although

I still loved her very much. I was also rebelling in mild, secretive ways (drinking, staying with friends, smoking).

Ex-boyfriend's suicide

From 15-17, two major events happened in my life. My first boyfriend committed suicide after our break-up. I had seen it coming, but was too young to understand how to deal with his problems. Guilt beyond belief followed, though rationally I understood it wasn't my fault. His suicide also left me a lasting attribute of watching people carefully for mental illness. Secondly, my school sent me to a therapist. The therapist said I needed to leave home because of my mother's mental illness, which I risked being sucked into. I'm not sure where I got the courage or the dispassion to leave, but I moved in with my second boyfriend. I felt guilty most of my life over this decision, but am beginning to realize that my mother may have needed to have me leave so she could allow herself to totally break down. I may have made the right decisions, but paid an emotional price in both instances. I was still drinking, but my new boyfriend was a brother-figure who stopped me from smoking or taking serious drugs. I think I chose him to stop my wild behavior. I visited my mother until she died. I never lost contact.

From 18-21, I studied psychology and feminism, trying to make sense of my life. I spent a lot of time blaming men in general and my father in particular for my mother's mental problems. It was not until I novelized the experience that I realized my father had done his best. I became a political lesbian for a while and ran "rap groups." When I graduated from college, I went to work in a mental hospital. I was always responsible even in the context of sex, drugs, and rock 'n roll. But I was not very happy.

Writing this, I realize that my reaction to the insanity I encountered was to try to reason my way out, to understand the roots of mental illness. —Jaki

Tom's Alcoholic Mother

My father died when I was 12 and my mother slipped further into her alcoholism. Within two months of his death, I moved from a life of considerable affluence to one of poverty. I was essentially orphaned, even though there were some significant other adults in my life who helped me—in particular, my only living grandparent.

Depressed and fatherless

I was a cute guy and plenty smart, so I always had girlfriends and always did well in school (even though my mother took no interest). Most of the friends I chose in high school were like me: fatherless and poor. But these were fairly strong bonds. I was quite clinically depressed, although I had no idea that I was, had no idea there was such a thing as depression. I had to do everything for myself, including earning all my money for clothes, car, entertainment. I became extremely self-sufficient, the downside to that being I learned never to ask anyone for anything.

Sex

For a kid in the early 1950's I became sexually active before most of my peers did. Sexuality was one of the few areas in which my self-esteem did not suffer. Never having any doubt, worry, or concern about my sexual self was a saving grace because I was mostly very unclear about who I was or who I was becoming. I made choices compulsively, desperately, with little or no consideration of the consequences. This quality led to a number of interesting adventures, but not much that was helpful in climbing out of the black hole of adolescence.

Adolescence as cover-up

I was seen as fairly cool, but that was achieved at huge expense to myself. The central metaphor for many adolescents is The Cover-up. And when The Cover-up results in a headlong flight from Essence (one's true self), it is directly responsible for much teenage angst and pain. —Tom

Alan Did It Alone

I call my adolescence benign neglect. I had to figure it all out by myself. I found my life a bit depressing: my mother was a clinging 4-Romantic and my father was an absent 7-Adventurer. I became a substitute husband for my mother in a way. So I tried to avoid her. My father never told me personal stories about himself. Neither was well educated, while I was academically destined and they couldn't understand me.

My parents were nice enough, though. They fed me and let me use their car. Their neglect was that they didn't offer any assistance to me—they didn't know how to support me or give me models. I went to Columbia University in New York City. My father offered to let me take over his business but he didn't pressure me, which was the good part. —Alan

Drawing from "The Career Within You" by Wagele and Stabb. Harper Collins.

Liz and Her Father

I felt way more grown up from the age of 10 than before. Puberty was starting and my body changing shape gave me concern. By 14 my hips seemed huge, though I don't think they were by objective standards. At around 14 or 15 I would get depressed and think, what's the use? I'd cry, feel desperate, and be angry with my father with no specific reason. These feelings gradually faded by the time I was 16 or 17 and thinking ahead to going to college.

I looked forward to being grown up beginning when I was maybe five or six, though I couldn't imagine ever getting there. I saw becoming self-sufficient as a gift and a kind of revenge to those who had power over me at that young age. My best defense was to hide. I'd fade into the background and watch what was going on, hoping to learn something. I wanted to be strong and independent, yet I was shy and doubted my ability to achieve this. I married my soulmate at age 19. I'm sure I did the right thing by marrying Gus, yet living alone for a few years before marriage would have been an advantage in terms of my maturity. —Elizabeth Wagele

Hard Worker Ernie

I was a farm boy in Michigan. I worked before and after school from an early age and seven days a week so I rarely played with toys. One or two Sunday afternoons a year we would take off if company was coming over. I drove the tractor from age 11 on. In the summer and fall months I would even take off from school to get the crops harvested. We'd be using the tractor 24 hours a day. I left home at 14, moved in with my cousin, and found a job in a grocery store. I eventually became a doctor. —Ernie

He Started Out Happy: "7 FIVE 7"

Back in pre-school days I was very sociable, adventuresome, curious, and optimistic. I loved kindergarten. We sang, danced, learned about reading and numbers, and played all these wonderful unisex games. I was more like a 7 (Adventurer), but maybe most children at that age are like 7's since life's adjustment problems haven't yet begun.

Out of step

First grade at a country school was a different story. During recess the boys were congregated at one side of the playground, the girls at the other. The boys were either playing a modified form of football or a war game in which you pretended that you were a B-29. World War II had begun a year before. These games made no sense to me, and the boys seemed neither welcoming nor friendly. I moved toward the center of the playground and observed the girls who were playing all the games I knew in kindergarten. I realized at that moment that I was somehow out of step with the world of children. The classroom was a different matter. I loved learning and always knew the answers. I immediately started some "learning projects," as my mother called them, at home: maps, geography, vocabulary, reading, piano, golf, and so on. Living in the country made me quite isolated but I didn't mind it. It was always wonderful when friends or relatives of my parents came to visit. I was well-behaved in the classroom except once when I started asking a teacher too many questions about an outline she was writing on the blackboard. Response: "You are always criticizing." After that I tried to be more diplomatic when I made comments or asked questions.

Curious about sex and homosexuality

In seventh grade I transferred to an elite public junior high school in the city, but continued living in the country. The only thing I didn't like was gym class. I joined the library club and was put in charge of shelving and noon desk. I was mostly alone in a 6,000-volume library for the noon recess.

I was in paradise. I read about one book a week (mostly classical novels) in addition to my long homework assignments. I was curious about sex and knew the magic call number 636. I read the two books from that section but they didn't tell me anything I didn't know. At the public library downtown, I sought the 636 books, only to see them through a locked glass case. I was afraid to ask where the key was. I did, however, find an interesting book called *You and Heredity*. There was a chapter about homosexuality, which I read several times. I had never heard the word before, but all I could gather was that many male homosexuals had feminine interests and were fat in the wrong places. That seemed to resonate with me. I looked the word up in the dictionary—it was the same as an "invert," another term I didn't understand.

Attracted to men

Some time in the next year I had a minor experimental session with an older neighbor boy whom I wasn't supposed to play with and learned what really attracted me. Furthermore, I was having more and more dreams and fantasies about sexuality, which left no doubt in my mind what my natural inclinations were. When I was in ninth grade, I saw a copy of *Coronet* magazine on a newsstand. A special white band was wrapped around it. "Homosexuality: New Moral Menace for Teenagers." I bought it and read it. The message was that homosexuals often lived in groups in larger cities and were supportive of each other as far as jobs and social connections were concerned, but that it was like a Mafia culture. Very depressing.

Military school

My parents sent me to military school for tenth grade because I was too isolated and needed to befriend boys of my own age. In the spring prior to my entrance to the school, there was a promotional dinner in my hometown, sponsored by the school. I was seated next to a cadet named David. He was exceedingly attractive, sophisticated, and very friendly. Because of this, I had very positive expectations of the military school. When I started the following September, I was assigned to room with someone from my hometown who was a fountain of information on all matters hetero- and homosexual. I mentioned having met David the previous spring at the banquet and wondered why he wasn't there. My roommate explained that he had tried to organize orgies or some such thing and consequently was asked to leave. I heard endless tales about what was going on with cadets who were currently at the school or had been there in previous years. Sex of all kinds was a common topic of dinner table conversation. Since I was oriented toward achievement and good conduct, I said no to all this temptation and simply enjoyed the vicarious pleasure of hearing about it.

I was so well prepared academically that I made straight A's in the academic subjects with minimal study. However, I was challenged in military and made a C in that subject. The following summer I returned home and worked on survival skills. I took typing lessons so I could be company clerk, I got coaching in riflery, worked part time in my father's office, and spent hours studying the military manual. No novels! I actually placed in the citywide junior golf tournament. I was promoted rapidly in the next two years, made friends, and eventually became a cadet officer. The latter wasn't so easy, because I had to discipline boys of my own age who were much tougher than I was. I realized I wasn't cut out for military life.

Like-minded individuals

I attended an Ivy League college and found that military school education didn't prepare me too well. Now I had to study hard to make mediocre grades. I also felt socially isolated. I took a psychology course, which discussed conditioned learning (Skinner boxes, shocks, rewards, etc.).

Someone asked the professor if this was a suitable technique for treating homosexuality. He replied that he would not recommend that for such a condition. He would advise the person to move to New York where there was a community of like-minded, supportive individuals. That certainly made sense to me. Some time later when I was feeling frustrated about my lack of academic achievement and my social maladjustment, I decided to get on the train and go to New York for the weekend. When I got off at Grand Central Station and saw all those people, none of whom I knew, I felt a surge of power and excitement. Nobody knows me. I can do whatever I want. The adventure began. Hello 7 (Adventurer), and if lust has anything to do with it, hello 8 (Asserter). Over the next couple of years, life became much more fun. I was very lucky because I did meet some wonderful people, some of whom became genuine role models for me. Grades improved; I felt I had a future. —Andrew

Part III: The Observer and the Seven Goals

1. **Developing the habit of doing tasks around home and good study habits** (see #5). As a 5, you probably already have good study habits.

2. **Being mindful of your body.** Observers who are introverted, as most are, may not be as interested in the image they present as most other types are.

3. **Being mindful of your social life.** Sometimes Observers encourage themselves to make friends because they know it's good for them, even when they must get away from their personal interests to do so.

4. **Being mindful of your emotional/spiritual development.** Connect to your 4-Romantic wing to help develop your spiritual side (if you don't already have a strong 4 wing) and connect to your 7-Adventurer arrow when you want more fun and excitement. Your 8-arrow can help you get out into the world.

5. **Nurturing your intellect.** You are probably already attracted to logic, problem solving, and finding out information.

Your Learning Style

- Most Observers are thinking types, which means you prefer the world of science, computers, the intellect, and so on. Some are feeling types, however, and may lean toward the Romantic personality. Most Observers are introverted, dislike conflict, and prefer working alone or with a small group.
- Make sure your learning environment is quiet. Though there are exceptions, most Observers are bothered by loud noise or other distractions.
- Avoid taking classes where you think you'll become impatient with too much time spent building rapport or you don't feel challenged enough.
- You are probably good at creating your own structure and going at your own pace.
- You might profit from getting involved in activities outside of regular school hours, such as clubs.

6. **Developing interests based on your passions and values.** Observers focus in depth on what they're interested in. They often like computers, science, math, music, and/or writing—something they can learn more and more about. Some excel at ordering information, for example in the library.

7. **Educating yourself on career choices** that incorporate your innate strengths, which include an ability to grasp structure, to focus, and to be objective. Observers have an original way at looking at the world.

What interests you—being a management consultant, educational researcher, physician, computer scientist, architect, photographer, engineer, attorney, mathematician, or something else? If your strengths differ from your passions (see #6), develop them both.

Part IV: What I Like about being an Observer

Part V: Healing Words

Fear paralyzes... Curiosity empowers. Be more interested than afraid.
—Patricia Alexander

Weird is just a side effect of being awesome.
—Author unknown

Sometimes one creates a dynamic impression by saying something, and sometimes one creates as significant an impression by remaining silent.
—Dalai Lama

A shy failure is nobler than an immodest success.
—Kahlil Gibran

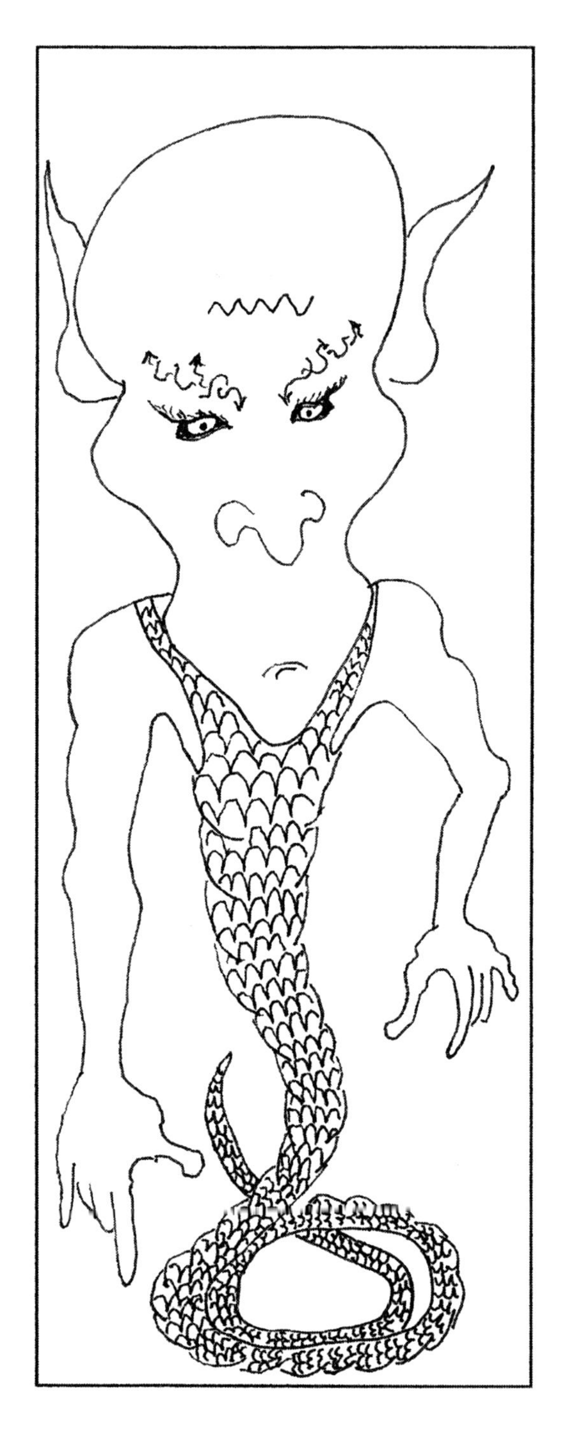

What's the best way to react if someone bullies you?

The 9 types say:

1: "Show him the error of his ways."

2: "Convince him to use his heart."

3: "Intimidate him so it won't happen again."

4: "Show him he *does* have some humanity."

5: "Be so strong in your inner world it doesn't bother you."

6: "Scare him off."

7: "Charm him out of it."

8: "Tell him, 'Go away!'"

9: "Turn it into something positive."

Enneagram Type 6 – The Questioner

A pessimist is one who feels bad when he feels good for fear he'll feel worse when he feels better. —Anonymous

Part I: Are YOU a Questioner?

Ambience: Watchful and sometimes high-strung

Attire: May like to dress in black

Good at: Scanning for danger; humor; being good detectives

Good with: Sometimes one person, sometimes good at entertaining groups

Noise level: Big range

Take away: Alertness, compassion

Influences: Questioners are influenced by their wings on each side of their number, the 5-Observer and 7-Adventurer. They are also influenced by the two types connected by lines, called arrows. The 3-Achiever and 9-Peace Seeker arrows can be used for growth, for example when the Questioner wants to act with confidence (3) or become more easy-going (9). See the Enneagram diagram in the Preface.

Questioner quiz based on statements by adolescents

Which of these ten sentences do you agree with?

Description

☐ I want to be safe and to be told the truth. —Jasmine

☐ I notice dangerous things that many people ignore. —Jose

The sky is falling

- ☐ I am aware of when people try to flatter me to get me to do things. —Sara
- ☐ I like to know what to expect. —Paul

What's the worst thing that can happen to a Questioner?

- ☐ Betray me, lie to me, or talk behind my back. —Jasmine
- ☐ Sometimes my imagination gets away from me. What I worry about happening has been worse than anything that's really happened to me. —Jasmine

What can you learn?

- ☐ Not to be such a people pleaser and crowd pleaser. —Lily Pearl
- ☐ I'm working on showing respect for my friends and other people. —Lily Pearl

How do you keep your boundaries?

- [ ] My parents were always worried I'd make a nuisance of myself so they didn't teach me to stand up for myself. Consequently I have poor boundaries. —Lily Pearl

- [ ] I am good at scaring people away. —Paul

You're a Questioner if you checked five or more of these boxes and identify with more cartoons and interviews in this chapter than in the other chapters.

Famous Questioners include: Adele, Eminem, Anne Hathaway, Diane Keaton, Jennifer Lawrence, Marilyn Monroe, Julia Roberts, David Letterman, George on *Seinfeld*, and Bruce Springsteen.

Drawing from "The Career Within You," Wagele/Stabb, HarperCollins.

Part II Being a Questioner

Jose Likes Safety

I'm always thinking. I like it when everything is crystal-clear. I don't trust my little sister because with her something will go wrong. Sometimes I worry all night long, especially about my future and doing well in school. I'd like to be a detective when I grow up. —Jose

The light at the end of the tunnel may be an oncoming train.

Skeptical Jasmine

I want to be safe and to be told the truth. I question almost everything and I try to avoid danger. But my friend who's also a Questioner challenges danger and takes chances. I think you can learn a lot by asking questions, although there are times when it is best not to. It takes a lot to earn my trust. I worry about people talking about me behind my back. This all might be because 5's, 6's, and 7's have fear issues. I don't believe you can group yourself into one number. I am all the numbers plus more. —Jasmine

Holly's Questions

Some words that describe the Questioner are defensive, anxious, testy, reliable, friendly, cautious, loyal, honest, controlling, strong-minded, wanting to be safe, and hyper-vigilant. Hyper-vigilant means we always want to know what's going on around us.

Around people, especially my parents, I like to know what is going on and what they are talking about. Here is a list of examples:

- Whenever I am asleep and there is a noise coming from outside my window I wake up and see what it is.
- Whenever I am sitting with my friends I always listen to their conversations.
- I hate it when people lie to me.
- Whenever I see people I know I wave and say hi.
- Whenever I am going somewhere I pack extra clothes just in case.
- Whenever I forget something I hate myself because then I don't feel secure.
- I am on swim team and when I dive into the water and my goggles fall off I have to stop and fix them.
- I get in trouble with my parents because I ask so many questions. — Holly

Paul and Humor

I was a wise guy in my all-boy high school. I enjoyed making the other boys laugh by making remarks when the teacher was writing on the board. I'd make devastating comments about things he said. He was an authority and an old guy and we were young guys.

When I was with my buddies, I would yell at people on the street for fun or throw oranges out the window and hope they would land on the hood of a car. I wanted to see the drivers' surprised faces. This was *counter-phobic* behavior: acting tough instead of scared or *phobic*.

Girls

I felt awkward with girls. I didn't know how to get from normal interactions to making out with them. I'd break up with someone, then have to go through the awkwardness all over again until I felt comfortable with someone new.

Teasing

I was a combination of someone who was good and responsible and a hurtful person. I wanted to be independent and to buy a car so I worked on a milk truck and delivered papers. I liked to tease but wasn't aware of how it felt to the person being teased. I was impervious. It seemed acceptable for us boys to make fun of each other. It even felt liberating to call a fat person fat, because that was reality. —Paul

Lily Pearl's Two Cultures

The effect my parents had on me (maybe) wasn't always, per se, the best but I'm sure they had my best interests at heart.

Mother kept me young

I started coming into my own about age 13 or 14. I think my mother wanted to keep me as a child and she used to say I was getting "fatter" and "bigger" and this was, in a way, not natural. She cried when I got my period like I had done something wrong. I cried too! My mother finding it hard to accept I had grown up affected my development generally. By growing up I was upsetting her.

Eating disorder

What my mother was saying affected my confidence, assertiveness and ability to accept the way I looked. I don't know whether my mum worrying I was getting fat and the subsequent development of an eating disorder were related. During university, I developed an eating disorder at one stage where my weight dropped to near seven stone (seven stone is 98 pounds)—I am 5 foot 4—but it was only for a year.

I felt the eating disorder stage was more of a way of controlling some aspect of my life as opposed to wanting to lose the weight. After I accepted that I could no longer keep up the punishing exercise routine and effective self-induced starvation, I started to accept the way my body would look. I am still not totally confident about this issue even to this day.

Chinese culture and self-esteem

In Chinese culture, the default position is one of modesty. If somebody complimented your daughter that she looked pretty, the thing to say would be "no, your daughter is way prettier." Obviously, this is polite but I don't think it helped my self-esteem, especially when I was the first daughter mentioned! When a distant aunt tried to compliment my mum on me being an obedient kid, my mum went on a ten-minute soliloquy rant as to why I was actually annoying. She was half venting but also trying to be polite and modest. She didn't realize I could hear her from my room and this really upset me.

People-pleasing

It was tough because at the age of 15 – 18, I was known in my friendship group as the "people pleaser." Kids at that age can naturally take advantage. "I can only choose four friends to go to Alton Towers with me, I won't choose her, she won't mind." Or "get her to give you a lift, or pay for your drinks, she won't mind." This led to me developing lower self-esteem, low confidence, low conceptions of self-worth, and other issues. I didn't know how to stand up for myself. Who would have taught me?

Bullying

When I was 18 and was about to leave school, my group of friends effectively turned against me and this other girl. It's one of those really long and terribly lame stories where you just look back and think, what was our problem back then? Why were we so immature arguing about stuff so unimportant? One of the girls started spreading rumors that I had harassed her aggressively for money. This wasn't as hurtful as the fact that other people believed her. Anybody who knew me should have known I would have never done anything of the sort. People started saying I was a bitch right before I was leaving for university. Because I felt I had left on such bad terms or in such a bad light, I only see a couple of people from high school now. This affected my social development because I had based my entire adolescence on being nice and people pleasing. I should have been more assertive from the beginning because at the end of the day, people will think what they want to think of you. I know this now, but not at the time and not for a long time after. Further, when all this was kicking off I didn't really have anybody to talk to.

University

I didn't have a good group of friends whom I could trust and who liked me, until I reached university. The change was really noticeable. In the first year, when I was getting to know everybody I overcompensated by doing everything for everyone, cleaning our communal kitchens, and always being the one to buy loo paper (toilet paper) and milk, etc. As I got more comfortable with them and trusted them more, by the second and third year our student house was a lot messier, shall we say!

I came into my own at university once I had decided on a degree I liked and I could see myself getting somewhere. I was lucky in finding a group of friends and still keep in contact today. Some of the things we used to argue about as a group of girls seem immature and insignificant now, such as boys or things people said. I never thought that at the time! Guess that's all emotional development.

Drugs and being paranoid

Although I had fun at university, I did get introduced to drugs (cocaine) in a big way during my final year and this stunted my development, on reflection. I was not learning how to deal with a long-term solution but always looking for a quick fix. It got quite bad at certain stages where I would say I was addicted. I started hallucinating and imagining I could hear sounds and was paranoid but I can only see that now; at the time, I genuinely thought the way I was thinking was the truth. But if you start, it is very difficult to stop. Also, the people who are usually doing drugs are also not true friends no matter how much you think they are at the time.

Relationships

People think being alone makes you lonely, but I don't think that's true. Being surrounded by the wrong people is the loneliest thing in the world.
—Kim Culbertson

When I had my first kiss at the age of 11 I didn't understand what was going on. I started dressing more sexily when I was 13 or 14. I saw my friends getting male attention and I wanted it too. When I didn't get it, I would take it badly. I used to have these intense feelings when I was 15 or 16 that I fancied someone or that he was the one for me. Looking back now, that could not have been further from the truth.

I didn't know how to control all these feelings. One month it was "I really fancy Bob," next month, "No, I really fancy Bill," next month, "No, Peter gave me his gloves during afternoon break—I fancy him." It consumed my life. I needed to know what they were doing and saying—trying to get some evidence they liked me. I was always the friend not the girlfriend though, in the end.

Lost virginity

I lost my virginity when I was 15. It was awful. I cried. I wasn't ready. But then, I proceeded to think I was going to marry the boy and we were going to run off together into the sunset to escape our lives, where nobody would find us. After that, I slept around. I know that sounds slutty. But I never would have described myself as a slut, per se. I never went out to look for it but I could never say no and was very easily flattered and led.

No self-respect

One sexual encounter pushed me up against a wall so hard I got a massive hole in my back from its rubbing against concrete (I was in a car park, yes, I know, classy bird!) and even then, I would say it was not okay to be mad at the boy for treating me in such a way. I had no concept of self-respect or self-worth. It's so important to teach young people today and young women, especially, that their life is valuable and they should be respected and respectful to others. It's important to give them the tools to deal with situations when they have been disrespected, including the confidence to say when it is not okay.

My first "proper" boyfriend wasn't suited to me. After that I continued to sleep around. I would get attached to people really easily. I found it difficult again to say no to any advances I'd get in a club; like I said, easily flattered, easily led. I think guys only needed to buy me a drink and I was theirs! I then went out with somebody who used to completely frustrate me with his incompetence but, again, thought I was going to marry him and we had a dead intense relationship. Both these relationships were relatively short—three to six months. Although, when people asked me how long I had been out with them for I would always say longer, as if having a long relationship in my life meant something?

I probably only started really emotionally developing after my first long-term relationship. This is tied to knowing myself more and understanding that the person I'm going to be in a relationship with needs to be right for me. This assessment is important and takes time. Life really isn't like in the movies; I believed wholeheartedly it was or could be.

Alcohol

Alcohol was very bad at this age in terms of increasing the number of self-respect-eliminating sexual encounters I had with boys. I will regret some of the bad things that happened forever. It took me a terrible amount of time to come to terms with it.

Lying

I used to lie because I was trying to hide something: how little attention I was getting off boys, if somebody had turned me down, or about my family background. I lied a bit at university to get attention. I definitely don't do it now but at the time, I did—so if you are 15 to 18 and you lie occasionally about random stuff, I used to do it too!

Work

My situation was unique, coming from a Chinese restaurant background—my dad didn't want me to follow in his footsteps: usually, they do! He would hate it when I helped out in the restaurant even when he needed it. However, I used to think sometimes I would have enjoyed it and would have been very good at it (considering my early experience and knowledge of how a restaurant is run), with maybe dreams of opening up a larger restaurant chain at one point.

College major?

I think there's a lot to be said for not going to university in England nowadays. Although because everybody goes to university, it does feel like having a degree is the status quo now! I know many people who have been successful and they did not go to university but started working when they were 16 or 17. At age 21, you may feel you did a degree because everybody else was doing it and then you come out and you're behind in life and commercial experience and in massive amounts of debt. —Lily Pearl

Loyal Sara

I belonged to a group of four to eight of the most popular girls in the 9th grade. A smart boy a year younger was dating one of the girls. One day he told me he'd carry my books if I wanted him to. He was pressured to go back to the girl he'd been dating, however, and so he did.

But the girls ostracized me for responding to his interest in me. Later, they formed a smoking club without including me. I was against smoking and drinking anyway. I rode my bike past the house where they met and looked in.

In the 10th grade a new girl came to our small town from the city of Chicago. She was different—she was witty, talked about Motown, liked to read, and played classical music. She was an outsider and not a churchgoer. I felt outside too and she validated me; in fact, she accepted me unconditionally. I became loyal to her. She went out with wild boys and sometimes I'd go along out to the cornfield to drink beer. I wouldn't have sex in high school because I knew if you got pregnant you'd never leave our small town. Two smart girls became pregnant and got married. I was attractive to boys so I had to be strong.

Anxiety

When I did creative things—I was passionate about writing, the theater, and performing—my anxiety would lift. I wrote features for the school newspaper, did skits for halftime at football games, and danced solos. The best part was connecting with the audience.

Idealism

In 8th or 9th grade I entered a speech contest and came in second. I had chosen a speech about the atom, nuclear power, and radiation, which I feared. I've always been very clear about my opinion against nuclear power. I also never took drugs. I was afraid they could hurt me.

Sometimes I withdrew and had immobilizing fear. My depression and dark thoughts were provoked by church dogma and years of exposure to a minister/Bible-school-teacher who attempted to frighten us into good behavior.

College

Away at college I began to question the authority of the minister. One of my professors especially encouraged this. I felt both freedom and uneasiness because of the change. I was in eleven plays in my first two years, then I used my own money to go to Paris and study at the Sorbonne. —Sara

I like feeling safe and protected

Drawing from "Finding the Birthday Cake" by E. Wagele. New Horizon Press

Part III: The Questioner and the Seven Goals

1. **Questioners are often energetic and hard workers**. An extra motivation for you to work hard may be to guarantee your need for safety and certainty.

2. **Most Questioners are mindful of their body.** You are likely to take a cautious approach to your health and safety and to work on having a sturdy, resilient body. Questioners often enjoy looking attractive and strong.

3. **Being mindful of your relationships.** Some Questioners especially feel safe by cultivating plenty of loyal friends.

From caring comes courage. —Lao Tzu

4. **Being mindful of your emotional/spiritual development.** Connecting to your 9-Peace Seeker arrow will help develop your spiritual side. You are most likely already compassionate.

Safeguarding the rights of others is the most noble and beautiful end of a human being. —Kahlil Gibran

5. **You are likely to already nurture your intellect** since you are naturally curious.

Your Learning Style

- Questioners tend to want to control their environment and like structure. Some are decisive and others have trouble making decisions. Since they are often thinking types, they often prefer the world of science, computers, the intellect, and so on. Some are feeling types, however, and prefer working with and around other people.
- You may lose interest if the learning material is too predictable.
- Cut down on your stress and anxiety by starting and finishing assignments as soon as possible instead of waiting until the last minute.
- You probably consider your teachers protective authorities and want to trust them, so try to establish good relationships with them.
- Consider studying in a study group where you give each other help and support.

6. **Developing interests based on your passions and values.** Questioners are often loyal, idealistic, and especially interested in helping and protecting the underdog. Some are interested in beauty and the arts.

Trust yourself...and you will know how to live. —Goethe

Loyalty

7. **Educating yourself on career choices** that incorporate your innate strengths, which include being exacting, skeptical, loyal, good at problem solving, witty, and the ability to fight for a cause. If your strengths differ from your passions (see #6), develop them both.

What interests you—education, business, science, math, engineering, information technology, manufacturing, healthcare, government or non-profit, law enforcement, literature, arts, entertainment, the food industry, the spiritual field, the military, the law, or something else? Whatever it is, you will bring alertness to your workplace.

Part IV: What I Like about being a Questioner

Part V: Healing Words for Questioners

Worrying is like walking around with an umbrella waiting for it to rain. —Wiz Khalifa

The ultimate authority must always rest with the individual's own reason and critical analysis. —Dalai Lama

Everything worth doing starts with being scared. —Art Garfunkel

The more you love your decisions, the less you need others to love them. Always listen to yourself first. —Anonymous

If a problem is fixable, if a situation is such that you can do something about it, then there is no need to worry. If it's not fixable, then there is no help in worrying. There is no benefit in worrying whatsoever. —Dalai Lama

Don't believe everything you think. —Anonymous

When I look back on all these worries, I remember the story of the old man who said on his deathbed that he had had a lot of trouble in his life, most of which had never happened. —Winston Churchill

THE ENNEAGRAM VALENTINE

Enneagram Type 7 – The Adventurer

When choosing between two evils, I always like to take the one I've never tried before. —Mae West

YOLO (you only live once)

Part I: Are YOU an Adventurer?

Ambience: Cheerful

Attire: Colorful

Good at: Lots of fun

Good with: Children, one-to-one, sometimes groups

Noise level: Often talks a lot

Take away: A desire to make the world a better place

Influences: Adventurers are influenced by their wings on each side of their number, the 6-Questioner and 8-Asserter. They are also influenced by the two types connected by lines, called arrows. The 5-Observer and 1-Perfectionist arrows can be used for growth, for example when the Adventurer wants to be more focused (5) or purposeful (1). See the Enneagram diagram in the Preface.

Adventurer quiz based on statements by adolescents

How many of these ten sentences do you agree with?

Description

- ☐ If I'm not doing something fun I'm desperately trying to find something to do that's fun. —Jade
- ☐ I have my down times but just about everything in my eyes can be fun in some way. —Diamond
- ☐ Any time something new comes up I at least look into it. —Nia
- ☐ 7's like to have tons of friends, but most of all to be the center of attention—at least me! —Malik

What's the worst thing that can happen to an Adventurer?

- [ ] Being bored and having no money. —Malik
- [ ] Making too many commitments you can't get out of. —Mary Beth

What can you learn?

- [ ] I get in trouble when I talk too much and too loud. —Jade
- [ ] I could use help learning how to finish things because I always have something else to do. —Lisa

How do you keep your boundaries?

- [ ] If people are talking about something I don't care about or don't want to talk about, I go talk to somebody else. —Jade
- [ ] It's no problem for me because I have known from the day I could talk I was going to be the boss! It's my 8-Asserter wing.—Lisa

Keep your face to the sunshine and you cannot see the shadow.
—Helen Keller

You're an Adventurer if you checked five or more of these boxes and identify with more cartoons and interviews in this chapter than in the other chapters.

Famous Adventurers include: Miley Cyrus, Tina Fey, Elton John, Shakira, Channing Tatum ("I just love to have fun..."), Robin Williams, and the characters James Bond and Indiana Jones.

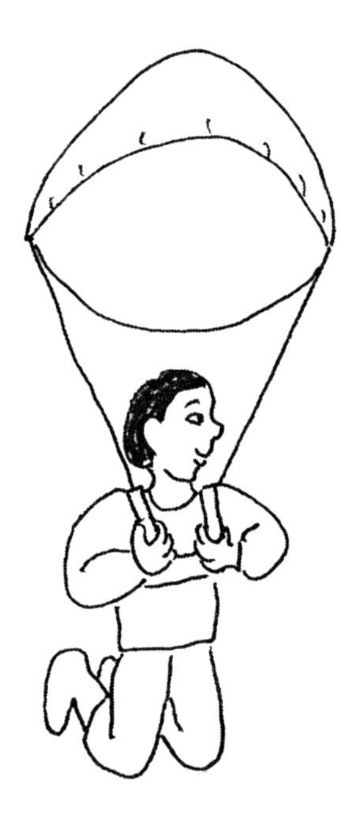

I can resist everything except temptation.

Part II: Being an Adventurer

Jade Hates Boredom

I am a 7-Adventurer because I'm always doing something. I absolutely hate being bored! If I'm bored that means I'm probably broke. I like being the center of attention and am always trying to make new and more friends—also, I get bored with people easily. Like if they're talking about something I don't care about or don't want to talk about, I go talk to somebody else. I'm always hyper. I sometimes get on people's nerves because I can be persistent.

Drawing from "The Enneagram of Parenting" by Elizabeth Wagele. HarperCollins.

I like trying lots of new things, like new carnival rides. I've always wanted to go bungee jumping and other exciting things. I also like to be talking most of the time. I have to be on the phone as soon as I get home from school. I get in trouble, like at school, at public places and lots of other places, because I'm always talking and I'm loud when I talk. I'm not like some people who just talk, talk, talk about nothing. I always have something to talk about like movies, TV shows, music, and lots of other stuff people like talking about. —Jade

Diamond and High Speeds

I am here to talk about the fun-loving, exciting life of a 7. I am always the first to do things. A good example is jumping my go-cart.

Sports

I love to go camping because there are tons to do. My dad always brings his quad/four-wheeler. He taught me how to work it last summer. I love the high speeds of knee boarding—the water against my face as I'm being pulled behind my friend's speedboat. The thing I hate most about camping is the long hours of fishing. Luckily I don't have to do it. I also like hiking and swimming. My friends also like to bridge-jump.

My favorite sport is gaming, a horse-oriented sport. The object is to ride around a course as fast as possible to beat other riders. I also have a dream of owning a world-class gaming horse and riding a bronco at a rodeo.

When I'm out of ideas or money I have to find something else I already love to do. At my house we have rollerblades and a skateboard I can use when it's not raining. I have a snowboard for when we go to a mountain. I also have horses to fill any gaps or when it's raining.

I want to try "the swing." It is two 150-foot poles with bungee lines connected to the top of them. The swinger is equipped with safety harness and helmet, then hoisted to the top and latched onto a bar with a pull and propelled far into the night. This attraction is in Reno, Nevada, in front of the Hilton Hotel.

I want to have a fast-moving, exciting relationship with a guy exactly like me. I have my down times, but just about everything can be fun in some way. —Diamond

Busy Nia

7-Adventurers are always busy, busy, busy. We enjoy doing new and adrenaline-pumping activities such as snowboarding or skydiving. 7's have a lot of energy and try many fun and exciting things. The sports and activities we stick to we do very well. We are social and friendly. Everything is planned out. The things generally disliked are being bored and being broke. Now I'll prove to you I'm a 7:

My schedule is as follows: Monday—Dance, PDE School, Homework. Tuesday—Dance, School, Homework. Wednesday—Dance, PDE School, Homework. Thursday—Dance, School, Homework. Friday—Pointe, School, Homework. Saturday—Dance, PDE. Sunday—Acting, Study.

When I'm not doing the scheduled stuff, I am doing regular every day pursuits. I can't stand being broke, although I am most of the time. Fun is my middle name and as you can see from the schedule one of my favorite hobbies is Dance. I would like to someday turn that hobby into a profession.

Any time something new comes up I at least look into it. I have many friends, young and old, and as far as I know they are friends back. —Nia

Lisa and Excitement

A 7-Adventurer is a person who always wants to be happy and will do almost anything to have fun. I usually have something to do that is exciting so I don't have to think about every other thing that is going on in the world. I cannot usually finish anything because I always have something else to do. I like to have lots of money so I can do all of the things I want.

What shows me I'm a 7 is that I love to go on the biggest, fastest, and scariest roller coaster ride there is! My family and I have done many things most people would not even think of doing! I would have to say "too bad for them" because they are missing out on so many exciting, thrilling breathtaking things! How many families would sit in a little seat 25 stories up in the air with nothing but space in front of them and know they will fall any time soon?

Wings and arrows also describe me. My 6-Questioner wing loves to be with people and have lots of friends. Questioners can handle the truth and hate to be lied to. When they're alone they get scared and feel unsafe. My other wing is the 8-Asserter, the boss or leader. They love to be in charge of things. When something goes wrong they think it was their fault and they need to fix it. I have known from the day I could talk I was going to be the boss!

The two arrows 7 points to are 1 and 5. The 1-Perfectionist has to have everything just right and in order. If they think something is wrong they will work for as long as it takes to make it perfect. I can't stand it being so messy, so some of the time when I am at friends' houses and their rooms are a mess I will clean them. When I see people at school with messy binders I will ask them if I can go through them and clean them out. My other arrow is 5-Observer, which means watcher. These people know a lot about people because they will just sit and watch. They like to be alone most of the time. —Lisa

Malik Has Fun

"Adventurous! Full of fun! Sounds like me!" I said. My friends at lunch had already been asking everyone, "What number are you? "I'm a 1-Perfectionist!" "You're a 1, I'm a 5-Observer!"

I had no clue what they were talking about until I got into Language Arts Class and we talked about the Enneagram. I learned the 7 meant happy, full of fun, doesn't want to see problems with the world. The worst thing for a 7 is being bored and having no money. 7's like to have tons of friends, but most of all to be the center of attention—at least me!

Sports

7 fits me because just the other day my friends and I were wrestling, and my friend slammed me on my back and cracked some of my ribs. And because I was so happy and hyper one day I went on my neighbor's rope swing and fell about 40 feet into sticker bushes.

And now that I realize how weird I am, I think there should be a crazy category just for me. —Malik

Optimistic Colin

Indiana Jones was always ready for adventure and fun. He always wanted to try new, fun, daring things. I bet he'd be a 7.

A 7 wants to laugh in the face of danger. Believe me, we have our faults, too. We always try to replace old, boring real-life things with fun exciting things. Also, we try to make ourselves believe life is going better than it really is.

I'm proud of being a 7 though, even with my faults and good qualities because we all have our good and bad sides. —Colin

Ron's Happy Childhood

I'm a 58-year-old Adventurer with a 6-Questioner wing and I'm an extravert. I haven't grown up yet—all my responsibilities will come later in life. I like the spur of the moment and having many, many options. I never wanted to be tied down and I'm always wondering what it would be like to live somewhere else. I constantly gather data and ask others' opinions to help me be sure I've made the *right* decision. I also want to understand. For example, if I give a presentation and 100 people like it but one doesn't, I have to find out why.

I want people to get along so I work the middle and try to find commonality. I'm not interested in being the one in control.

Work

Dad didn't get beyond high school. My mother taught high school business: accounting and bookkeeping. Having a paper route and collecting money from customers led to the idea that maybe I'd be an accountant—how about for a rock and roll band? Then I could have the adventure of traveling with them.

My older brother was the "smart one" in the family. I was surprised when my mother showed me my report cards and I had gotten straight A's. I had a scholarship to college but instead of taking it, I left my small town of McCook, Nebraska, and played in the Rocky Mountains around Boulder, Colorado, skiing and hiking for five years. I earned money as a hod carrier for the bricklayer father of a friend of mine. I also worked in an IBM warehouse as a forklift operator.

In 5th grade, my friend's older brother had a newspaper route. We wanted to make money too, so we split a weekly advertising paper route. I liked being an explorer and going to all the parts of town to deliver papers. I also liked the concept of working for myself. So I got a daily newspaper route and always had money for the weekends. I would visit the hobos down at the railroad tracks and listen to their stories. Eventually I delivered my newspapers from a motorcycle, which gave me the sense of entitlement and independence.

After Boulder, a neighbor of ours in Nebraska gave me a job working for the railroad at a good wage as a computer keypunch operator. I didn't take the job seriously because I wanted to explore the world. Then I worked for a train derailment company. We covered eight states and a 500-mile radius of my hometown, and immediately my "world" expanded. It could be exciting to dive into lakes and rivers for derailed trains. I wanted to skydive and parachute, too. After a year-and-a-half I went back to Boulder, then on to college.

I never wanted to push people to buy something and I didn't want to go into construction. Now I work in the hospitality industry, where I get to meet interesting people and hear stories.

Sports

At 14 I was on the swim team, played summer baseball, and was on the high school basketball team. I also did the trampoline and the pole vault in track. I liked having a solo sport. I didn't want to play football because I didn't like physical contact and getting hurt. In the summers I was a lifeguard at the public pool and could use the diving board over the five-minute breaks to show off. I was good at doing twists and backflips.

Idealism

At 24, I thought I should go to college. A four-year degree seemed necessary to get a good job, so I went to the University in Lincoln, Nebraska. I majored in accounting and it took me twelve years to graduate at the age of

36. School was safe and I didn't have to commit to girlfriends and careers. "I'm a student. I haven't graduated yet! Marriage, family, and career can come later." I explored the philosophical side of things and began reading.

Later, I went back to college and got an M.A. in Christian Spirituality in Berkeley, California. I wanted to get a firm footing in Western Christian religion and then study Eastern religions to find their commonalities. I investigated spiritual voices of our times and went to a lot of monasteries. Silence and the contemplative tradition interested me.

Happy family life

My mother and father and two sets of grandparents living in the same town were always there for me as a child. I also had close aunts, uncles, and cousins. We four kids would go to Grandma's house to wait after school until Mom got home. I was never afraid to work. We were taught good values, such as honesty, responsibility, and the value of money. As a 7, however, when I received my college loan each semester I spent half of it right away.

My parents treated all four of us equally. There was never any abuse of any kind. The most important thing for me is that our parents never told us what to do—they wanted us to follow our own dreams. —Ron

Mary Beth, the Reader

I loved my teachers in junior high school: the Latin teacher who lived near the U.C. campus with her husband and pet monkey, the kind math teacher, Miss Alma, and the slightly crazy science teacher who lived at the Claremont Hotel. I was asked to join something they called a "sorority" and freaked out because it felt way over my head in terms of committing to something, so I didn't even consider it. The fellow students I remember liking were a Chinese boy and Japanese girl, maybe because my elementary school had been very white.

I moved to another town when I started high school, which I thought was way too suburban, although I didn't have that word yet. I wanted to fit in and did hang out with girls I liked who thought they were hot stuff. But I worried about how much they really liked me. I made a decision to try to stop thinking about what people thought so I could think more about my own self. I think I must have been fairly self-absorbed and not particularly mature, although I was responsible.

Boys

I had a few crushes in elementary school but none I remember in junior high. In high school, I wanted dates and to go to dances. I did get two steadies, one of which dumped me hard, which left me pretty devastated for a while. I then went for his best friend, whom I had liked better anyway. I spent much of my time pining away for a bigger life and reading about faraway places and other lives. I thought my present circumstances were temporary and my life would lead to bigger things. I was critical of many of my contemporaries and would have liked to be more appreciated (asked out on dates, to parties, voted most something, named editor of the paper).

Family life

My family life was pretty easy and I remember being pretty happy if a little overly introspective. Later I found out my family thought I spent a lot of time in my room, mostly reading, but I thought it was normal. I wasn't that worried about my looks, although I recognized that others were a lot better looking. I tried to fit in with clothes but am not sure if I did well or not.

Felt alone

I was religious until I was 20 and talked to God a lot, which I found kind of stimulating in my self-absorbed way. I did feel alone and that no one really knew what was in my head. I longed to be able to share more intimately my "unique" thoughts, but felt I didn't know how most of the time. I think feeling separate was the worst part. I had always felt my mother was interested in herself and her husband mostly, and I didn't yet know how to connect with others. —Mary Beth

Part III: The Adventurer and the Seven Goals

1. **Developing the habits of using time wisely and balancing your activities** (see #5). Use your Perfectionist arrow for discipline if you need help with this.

2. **Being mindful of your health**. Being sociable and active, you probably already do well on this goal. Adventurers often have an interest in keeping the earth a healthy and attractive place, too.

3. **You are probably already mindful** of your relationship to your friends, parents, siblings, community, and teachers.

4. **Being mindful of your emotional/spiritual development.** Adventurers often feel nurtured by music, nature, and being busy. You most likely already feel life is magical.

5. **Nurturing your intellect and logical thinking.** Adventurers usually like to read books on many subjects.

Your Learning Style

- Adventurers like flexible learning environments or they tend to feel too confined.
- Make sure there is fun and action in your learning environment.
- Set short and realistic goals.
- Pick and choose from a rich learning environment if possible.
- Study in several sessions rather than one.

6. **Developing interests based on your passions and values.** Make note of which ones are most important to you.

7. **Educating yourself on career choices** that incorporate your innate strengths, which include the ability to explore new ideas and activities, multitasking, networking, optimism, and playfulness.

What interests you—travel, science, the arts, the health field, construction, business, writing, journalism, or something else? You are unlikely to want a job with much repetition or boring times. If your strengths differ from your passions (see #6), develop them both.

I excel at networking.

Part IV: What I like about being an Adventurer

Part V: Healing Words for Adventurers

I find hope in the darkest days, and focus in the brightest. I do not judge the universe. —Dalai Lama

There are those who give with joy, and that joy is their reward. —Kahlil Gibran

Be in love with your life. Every minute of it. —Jack Kerouac

SUMMERTIME
AND THE LIVING IS EASY
Too small, little feller - back you go.
1
What would you like for lunch?
2
Schubert TROUT Processing Plant
3
I sing to thee O majestic Tuna of the deep-
4
My favorite kind of fishing expedition...
5
How do I know that factory isn't polluting the water?
6
I wish I had his optimism!
ICE HOCKEY TONIGHT
7
Get your tail outta my pond, Mister!
8
9
FISH ARE JUMPIN'
It's too deep for me...

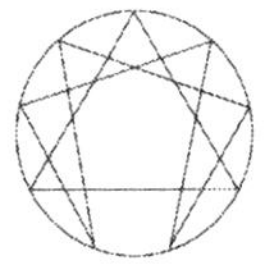

Never go to bed mad – stay up and fight.

Enneagram Type 8 - The Asserter

Part I: Are YOU an Asserter?

Enneagram Type 8 – The Asserter. "What's it to ya?"

Ambience: Can fill up the room with his/her presence

Attire: Anything goes

Good at: Telling it like it is

Good with: Children, one-to-one, sometimes groups

Noise level: Can be very loud

Take away: Often protective of others

Influences: Asserters are influenced by their wings on each side of their number, the 7-Adventurer and 9-Peace Seeker. They are also influenced by the two types connected by lines, called arrows. The 2-Helper and 5-Observer arrows can be used for growth, for example when the Asserter wants to develop his or her softer side (2) or focus on something intellectually stimulating (5). See the Enneagram diagram in the Preface.

*The difference between an 8-Asserter and a **6**-Questioner*
Drawing from "Are You My Type, Am I Yours?" Wagele/Baron. HarperCollins

Asserter quiz based on statements by adolescents

How many of these ten sentences do you agree with?

Description

- ☐ I enjoy leading groups and having it my way. —Desmond
- ☐ I think quick and from my gut. —James
- ☐ I will respect your strength as you will mine. —James
- ☐ I am independent, am sometimes a bully, have anger problems, and try to keep people in line. —Maria

What's the worst thing that can happen to an Asserter?

- ☐ For things to get out of control. —James
- ☐ To be disrespected. I will flip out. —Maria

What can you learn?

- ☐ Often we will tell it how it is and aren't respectful of other peoples' feelings. I can learn to be more respectful. —Desmond
- ☐ I need to find other ways to express my anger than on other people. —Jose

How do you keep your boundaries?

- ☐ Someone was playing his radio loud and I didn't like it. I looked him in the eye and said, "Go away." He stayed there with his radio playing. I repeated, "Go away." He left. —Joey
- ☐ When I want something really badly, my body focuses on that particular thing until I get it. —Joe

You're an Asserter if you checked five or more of these boxes and identify with more cartoons and interviews in this chapter than in the other chapters.

Famous Asserters include: Nicki Minaj, Avril Lavigne, Demi Lovato, Pablo Picasso, Pink, Mike Tyson, and Britney Spears.

Part II: Being an Asserter

These go from youngest to oldest—from adolescents now to adults recalling their adolescence.

Zane the Leader

I think I have been an 8-Asserter my whole life. I am always the leader. I am in charge.

I'll show you how to hunt.

Sports

Every time we play a sport at school or at home, the kids want to be on my team, and most of the time I am the captain. I always know what is going on at school—what is cool, and what isn't.

Even some of the older kids like me and follow me around. As I have gotten older, I've become more and more of a leader. I think that is one reason I make a good point guard in basketball.

At my house my room isn't always clean but I make sure nobody touches my stuff. Whatever I am doing with my family I made it a competition, even eating at the table!

Yes it's true, I'm an 8 in all ways, and sometimes I do get a little bossy and I have to have it my way. But sometimes that can be good. —Zane

Desmond the Competitor

An 8 is a person who loves to be in control. We are strong, energetic, and like challenges.

Sports

I love competing against people and I enjoy the feelings when I win. On one such occasion a kid thought he was a lot better than me at surfing. This made me angry. It just so happens that we were going to a surf contest together. He thought I was never going to beat him, but he had another thing coming. We both got to the finals and I beat him and got fourth. He came out sixth. I gloated forever about it.

There is only one thing I am not that an 8 is supposed to be, and that is strong. I am probably one of the weakest kids in the 8th grade.

I also enjoy leading groups, having it my way. I can't stand it when people try to take over a project and tell me how it is going to be done. I like people to just let me take control. One time in the 5th grade I did a group project on the planet Saturn. It could have been a fun thing, but one girl decided she would do the project all by herself. Before I knew what was going on she was painting Saturn hot pink. I started to freak out. In the end we got a "D" on the project and it wasn't my fault.

Being an 8 is awesome. I'm glad I did this Enneagram project and I know what I am. It taught me a lot about myself. —Desmond

James Fights Back

Respectful, independent, and athletic—that's me. The words above mean nothing to you if you have never heard of the Enneagram. It suggests what kind of person you really are.

In charge is the way of the 8-Asserter. Many people call us different because we are. The worst thing that can happen to an 8 is for things to get out of control. This is due to the factor that 8's are very picky. Things have to be done our way or no way. You need to be direct with me.

When I go to a party and my friends start messing around not doing what they are supposed to be doing, I become uncomfortable because things in my world become out of whack.

Sports

When my friends and I play basketball I always seem to turn into the ref and stop having fun. And afterward I feel bad for my friends just because they had to put up with me. During any sport if I see somebody doing the wrong thing, I become a coach. This is why I have limited amounts of friends.

Although my 8 friends seem annoying, they mean good just like me. The one bit of advice I can give is if you run into an 8, don't challenge them. They will fight right back almost instantly with no remorse. —James

Crusher Carlos

I'm a genuine, classic 8. I'm in charge. It's my way or the highway. Don't mess with my authority. If you make my life miserable, I'll take the challenge of making yours miserable as well. I won't give up until I succeed with this task either. If you're stronger than me, I'll work until I get stronger. If you put me in a stressful or tough situation, I'll glide my way through it with grace. I'll be straightforward with you. I'm a leader. My self-confidence will crush yours. Don't expect me to always make the right decision. I think quick and from the gut.

Perfectionists and Peace Seekers also come from the gut but in different ways. I express anger directly, Peace Seekers hide anger, Perfectionists are resentful because things aren't perfect enough.

I'll work until you tell me to quit, so don't think I need a break. Don't blame me for being stronger, for I will respect your strength as you will mine. Listen to what I have to say and don't think it can be any better cause it's the best.

Trouble with authority

All through my childhood I went through phases that I had to overcome with my own will and strength. One of these was my leadership ability. When I started school, children just began to listen. I had no control over it—it was just a gift from destiny. It carried its way through further years of school and would soon become a problem. When I began doing something, other students would follow. Teachers didn't approve of this so the blame had to come down on someone and that quickly became me. As you should have already assumed, this got me in more and more trouble each year. Soon I was having huge arguments with teachers and completely ignoring their authority. I then started seeing counselors to try to get even with teachers I thought didn't like me. I would be blunt and to the point by telling them no to all requests or suggestions. Every time the class would follow me, I'd grow even stronger in confidence. I would work harder at getting to the teachers I didn't like. If a teacher challenged me, I'd never give up and would be sent out of class. I would get students to follow me as well for fear I would be the only victim to put the blame on. My ignorance and confidence still made me believe I could fight the teachers I came across.

This problem will almost always be with me but I don't care. If I have improved greatly from then to now, then think of how improved I'll be in the future. Where this habit will get me in life I do not know. It's part of who I am. My whole family is an 8. I hope my kids in the future are 8's. So whether being an 8 is good or bad, it's the best to be to me, and I'm proud to be one. —Carlos

Maria's Hot Temper

The Asserter is the chief. I want to be boss, always the leader and in control. An 8 is independent, respected, sometimes a bully, has anger problems, and tries to keep people in line. 8's have the worst way to express anger.

I have always had a very hot temper. When somebody makes me mad I explode. My family is always mad. My brother is the one that makes me mad the most because he thinks just because he's bigger he can bully me around.

Little calf: "All I did was say Hi!"

One time last year, before the second time our house flooded on the river, my brother and I got into a fight. He was 20 years old and he wouldn't stop bugging me. I tackled him because he wouldn't stop. My uncle grabbed me off of him, but I broke loose and when I did my brother was already on his feet. I reached over and grabbed an apple and threw it at him. I missed him and hit the top of the stove.

Sometimes at my house I'm in the middle of doing something and someone wants me to do something else and I flip out and yell. I don't like getting mad but I always do when I'm in a bad mood and someone asks me to do something. I also hate it when somebody bothers me while I'm doing something else. Sometimes I get angry when my brother gets mad and takes it out on me. When someone asks me nicely to do something I will, but when they say it in a mean way I won't do it and I will get mad. —Maria

Decisive Jose

When something sad happens to me or someone else, I think with my gut. My stomach gets real tight. That's a good thing because it doesn't cloud my judgment.

We are called the chiefs or bosses because we like to be in control. In all the games and sports I play I want to control all the other players. If something goes wrong I feel it is my responsibility to get things back into place.

Sports

8's usually make the best athletes because they are determined to win and they do their best. Athletes make decisions quickly, even if they are not the right ones. They don't get confused easily because they stick with their decisions until proven wrong. Even when wrong they go down fighting.

8's can get into a lot of trouble. They need to find other ways to express their anger than on other people. That is why 8's are so unique in their different kind of way. —Jose

Joe Takes Charge

An Asserter is someone who can step in and take charge in some of the worse situations. They can make fast decisions, but sometimes they aren't thinking when they make them. Sometimes their bossiness makes people mad. They would rather give directions than receive them.

When a teacher puts me in a group with people who goof off a lot, I usually take charge. Sometimes I get bossy and make other people watch me while I work because I don't want them to have fun without me. And I don't want them to mess up the project.

Stubborn

When I was five years old I got really upset, like 8's can when they don't get their way. My mom made me wear this suit and tie because it was Easter and we were going to church. I didn't want to wear the suit, though, because at that time in my life I only wore shorts and T-shirts. When my Mom finally got the suit on me, I threw a huge tantrum. My face looks like a chili when I get mad. My mom was worried that I might pass out or something because when I get mad, even today, I stop breathing. She had to take me outside to cool me down. In the end I think I only half won because I got rid of the dress shirt and the tie. You have to admit though that you would have to put up a good fight in order for your mom to let you wear a T-shirt to church on Easter Sunday.

When I want something really badly, my body focuses on that particular thing until I get it. Nothing can stop me. I think that is typical of an 8. —Joe

Spunky Helen

Most of my friends were boys. I didn't really understand girls though I identified with boys. The constant fallouts and inane chatter from girls drove me insane! I just needed to keep things simple and I got that from boys. However, problems arose when boys fancied me. Three of my male friends and I were hauled into the Headmaster's office again for fighting between us. I liked that I could do this with them as it got rid of a lot of my pent up anger and aggression. However, according to the Head it was becoming a problem and we needed to sort it. The boys were asked to leave and me to stay. I remember feeling really angry thinking I better not be getting all the blame for this! The Head then asked me why I thought we were fighting, I replied we were having fun, though as they were bigger than me they did sometimes hurt me. I knew they didn't mean it. He asked me did I think they fancied me. I was shocked as that had never even entered my thoughts! When I asked the boys they told me, I was really good fun and great at lots of things that we all liked to do, like playing pool and darts, so they all really liked being with me. I am still really good friends with one of them, and he now tells me "Of course we all fancied you!" I felt my sexual side was only apparent to me and although I experimented with myself I wasn't happy to get involved with that side of things with my boy friends.

Drugs

Although I did dabble a little with drugs, I didn't really start to experiment with them until I was much older and wiser. I knew I pushed things to the limit and I felt I would do myself harm and get into even more trouble had I continued.

Acting out

I spent a lot of my adolescence having to stay at home as punishment because I got into trouble a lot. There were a few brushes with the law. When my week or month's reprimand was up my Mum would say, "I mean it, a minute after (whatever time I was told to be in) and you're in for another week." I would purposefully wait around the corner so I could be late because no one, not even my Mum, was telling me what to do! I would climb out of my bedroom window anyway and sneak back in.

School

I went to an all girls' high school from 13-16 years old. Spending any more school time with boys could have had a detrimental effect on me. However, I hated that school and played truant a lot; and got away with it a lot. I have since had to pay for my own education, though interestingly I don't regret that.

Sex

My Mum wanted me to be a lady. She would have even settled for me being a little girlie, though I only wore jeans or trousers with a top and trainers (there were many times I needed to run!) and I had a foul mouth. I loved being with and behaving like boys, and I was having so much fun. Although lots of people questioned my sexuality, I never did. I knew I fancied men and was interested in them sexually though having lots of male friends and having fun with them was so much more important to me than having a relationship.

My sexual exploits were kept well away from my friends and I would chuck those boys to the side once I had had my fun. Many of them in later life told me I broke their hearts. I had no idea, though at the time I really didn't care either.

Bold

I was the life and soul of every party and the person who made things happen out of all the different groups I dipped in and out of, and I loved that. People always wanted to see more of me though I needed to be constantly stimulated and I never got that from just one group.

I was always told, "You have the balls to say what everyone else wants to say though daren't." I loved myself for that! The fact I loved myself really annoyed people who didn't know me. I knew it and I would give them a mouthful saying, "It's not my fault you don't like who you are and that I piss you off! I'm not going to change to make you feel better." —Helen

Revan the Politician

I enjoyed my adolescence in England, a long time ago. There was no teenage culture there at all—no milkshakes, no dates, no sock hops. Schools were mostly of the same sex. This was true of most of the world. We teens didn't have cars and we weren't a sexually saturated atmosphere as in America. We didn't have alcohol until we were at least 17. After school we did homework, played athletic games, and went to movies. Radio was huge, too, and we repeated catchphrases from the comedians we heard there. Entertainment was the same whether you were 15 or 50.

It was a good time for me—there were few pressures. As an adolescent I was precocious politically. People expected I would become a hot-shot politician. I became the head of the Labor Party, the biggest political organization at Oxford University, and influential in British politics, from age 21-23. This could have led to a seat in Parliament. After this I served as honorary vice-president of the Labor Club at Oxford—I'm still the only student who has ever done this. —Revan

Part III: The Asserter and the Seven Goals

1. **Developing the habit of using time wisely and good work habits** (see #5). Most Asserters have a lot of energy. It can be a problem when they use it too much for having fun and don't learn how to work.

2. **Being mindful of your body and health**. This is an important goal for you since your lust for life could have a bad effect on your health. Stay aware of needing plenty of sleep and healthy food.

3. **Being mindful of your social life.** Connect to your 9-Peace Seeker wing if you want to become less overbearing. Asserters can be extraverts or introverts. Introverted 8's sometimes appear to be brooding.

4. **Being mindful of your emotional/spiritual development.** Connect to your 2-Helper arrow if you want to develop your gentle side more and connect to your 5-Observer arrow if you want help concentrating on reading or other quiet activities.

5. **Nurturing your intellect.** Asserters can become annoyed with people who aren't clear about the facts.

Your Learning Style

- You are probably decisive and focus on structure. 8's often prefer a logical approach to what they do.
- You may become impatient when too much time is spent on feelings and building rapport.
- Develop routines for the various tasks you want to do every day.
- Finish your learning tasks before anything else after school or you might not get them done. Think of pleasure and recreation as rewards.
- Anger can interfere with Asserters and school. Remember education is for your benefit, not the teachers' or the school's. Try to direct your anger to constructive ends (injustices) that don't slow down your progress.

6. **Developing interests based on your passions and values.** Passion for things often comes easily to Asserters. Try to keep a balance between your various interests. For example, if you love playing sports make time for other interests as well.

7. **Educating yourself on career choices** that incorporate your innate strengths, including the ability to enforce rules and protect others, negotiation skills, leadership skills, and standing up for justice. If these strengths differ from your passions (see #6), develop them both.

What interests you—sports, healthcare, science or technology, becoming an air-traffic controller or an executive, the law, or law enforcement? Whatever it is, keep in mind that many Asserters are happiest when working for themselves.

Part IV: What I Like about being an Asserter

Part V: Healing Words for Asserters

You have enemies? Good. That means you've stood up for something, sometime in your life. —Winston Churchill

Only those who will risk going too far can possibly find out how far one can go. —TS Eliot

Danger – if you meet it promptly and without flinching—you will reduce the danger by half. Never run away from anything. Never! —Winston Churchill

I'm not anti-social. I just have a strong aversion to B.S., drama, and pretending. —Anonymous

The Enneagram of Bathtubs

Enneagram Type 9 – The Peace Seeker

I always procrastinate when I get around to it.

Part I: Are YOU a Peace Seeker?

Ambience: Pleasant."I'm chillin'."

Attire: What blends in

Good at: Mellow conversation

Good with: Children, one-to-one, sometimes groups

Noise level: Not loud but sometimes has trouble knowing when to stop talking

Take away: Known for having a generous spirit

Influences: Peace Seekers are influenced by their wings on each side of their number, the 8-Asserter and the 1-Perfectionist. They are also influenced by the two types connected by lines, called arrows. The 3-Achiever and the 6-Questioner arrows can be used for growth, for example when the Peace Seeker wants to develop leadership skills (3) or engage critical thinking (6). See the Enneagram diagram in the Preface.

Peace Seeker quiz based on statements by adolescents

How many of these ten sentences do you agree with?

Description

☐ I don't like discomfort and don't like to make decisions. I avoid conflict and hate to have to say no to someone. —Luan

☐ I can see things from many points of view. —Luan

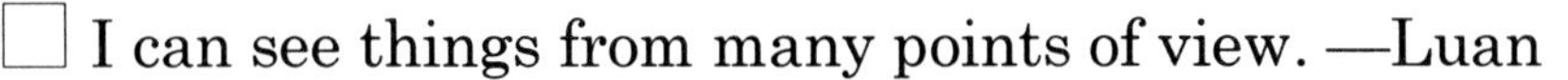

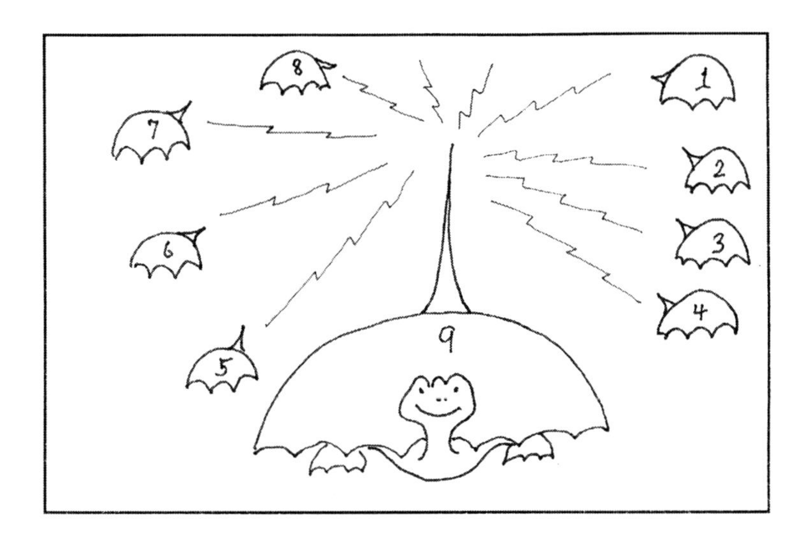

Drawing from "The Career Within You" by Wagele/Stabb. HarperCollins

☐ Although I go with the flow, I try to prevent confrontations. —Rosita

☐ Sometimes when I should feel bad or take action, I hide or just feel numb. —Naomi

What's the worst thing that can happen to a Peace Seeker?

☐ Having to make up my mind which of two incredible things to choose from in a very short time and I can only have one. —Luan

☐ Being around people who fight all the time and you can't do anything about it. —Rosita

What can you learn?

- ☐ I'm trying to figure out how to be less stubborn. —Rosita
- ☐ Sometimes I'm too concerned about making peace to take care of getting what I need for myself. —Bev

How do you keep your boundaries?

- ☐ Looking back, I would say no to doing things that violated my private self. I would say to those people, "I hope you understand. I don't feel like singing." —Naomi
- ☐ It's easier for me to help others keep their boundaries and stand up for their rights than to do it for myself. —Tyler

You're a Peace Seeker if you checked five or more of these boxes and identify with more cartoons and interviews in this chapter than in the other chapters.

Famous Peace Seekers include: Beyonce, Janet Jackson, Abraham Lincoln, Toby Maguire, Bruno Mars, and Rihanna.

Drawing from "Are You My Type, Am I Yours?" by Wagele/Baron. HarperCollins.

Part II: Being a Peace Seeker

These go from youngest to oldest—from adolescents now to adults recalling their adolescence.

Drawing from "Are You My Type, Am I Yours?" by Wagele/Baron. HarperCollins.

Luan Avoids Conflict

I like to keep things as they are. I don't like discomfort and don't like making decisions. I can be stubborn at times but I'm usually friendly. I can't even make up my mind which kind of ice cream I want. Just last week at the store I couldn't decide between German Chocolate Cake and Mocha Almond Fudge. Today I couldn't decide which personality I was. I am usually nice to everyone and say "Hi" to people who walk by unless they don't look like they're in the mood. Sometimes I have a hard time saying no. If people want me to hang out and I don't want to, I always come up with an excuse so I don't hurt their feelings.

Why has there never been a holiday where peace is celebrated all throughout the world? —Stevie Wonder

I see things from many points of view. It's funny that one person can have so many personalities: I always talk, I hate to be lied to, and I'll give you the cold shoulder if you lie to me. It takes a lot for me to show my anger though. I also like to be the best at school: I compete with my brother, if I fail at something I get very upset, I like to get everything right, and to be the leader in class groups for projects. I'm proud to be a Peace Seeker. —Luan

Rosita: Can't We All be Friends?

Well, I guess I'm a 9 although I have many traits from other numbers. Although I go with the flow and am laid back, I try to avoid or prevent conflicts and confrontations. I love to listen and help others with problems. I'm also considerate of others but can be pretty stubborn. Decision-making is a big problem for me because I'm afraid I'll make the wrong one and cause problems.

Parents fighting

I can never make a decision unless I take forever and even then I'm still afraid I'm wrong. When I was younger I hated it when my parents would fight. I think that's why I hate fighting so much today. It's important to accept other people.

When I was nine years old all my best friends moved away at the same time for two years. I was so lonely. So now I try to be nice, generous, honest, and caring because I don't want them to go. I'm a Peace Seeker because I don't want people to fight and because I think everybody should be friends with each other. —Rosita

There was never a good war or a bad peace. —Benjamin Franklin

Tyler Keeps the Peace

I'm fairly easy going; I get along most of the time with most people and I *really* don't like conflict. I like my life to run as smoothly as possible and don't like big changes in my routine. I hate it when my daily life gets switched around, even if it's only for a little while.

I often find it hard to say no. I like to make other people happy and it's at my own expense a lot of the time.

Rose-colored glasses

On one occasion two of my cousins were fighting over bicycles. They were throwing punches at each other when I yelled at them to stop. They stopped hitting but started throwing things at each other. I yelled at them again to stop and this time they did. I told them they needed to talk about it and they talked things out. We all sat down and played a game.

Forgetfulness is another of my traits. I have so much to do that I forget to do some of the things I need to do. This gets me in trouble with my mom sometimes. I'm peaceful, a little forgetful, and I like to make people happy. —Tyler

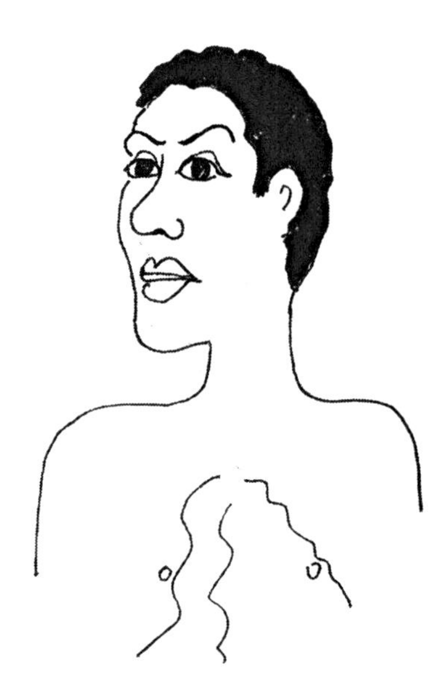

Nick and Body Hair

When I was 11 years old I got body hair on my chest and it drove me crazy. I didn't want anyone to see it. That's when I switched from taking baths to showers. I thought it was gross, like having leprosy or something. I didn't think about myself before this.

I thought I was ahead of most of the people I knew in getting this hair and it separated me from the group—it made me foreign. I wished everybody in my class would've gotten hair simultaneously.

As far as independence and a career were concerned, all I wanted to do in the 6th grade was to make movies, but I couldn't see a path to getting there at the time. —Nick

Bev's Alcoholic Parents

If I had known other kids also had alcoholic parents, life would have been easier. My father was an alcoholic. My mother was side-tracked and stressed out worrying about him. My grandparents helped me by just being there, and so did my aunts and uncles.

When I came to a new school in the 7th grade, I was put in low-achieving groups by mistake. I wasn't going to complain and it took the school a long time to correct my classes after my mother complained. The kids in my new classes (the same kids stayed pretty much in these classes until we graduated from 12th grade) had already bonded and I never regained my confidence. I was quiet and not comfortable with my opinions.

I worried a lot about my home life and never wanted my mother to be asleep when I returned from school. Unlike me, my sister was defiant but I always made peace. Playing sports gave me a place at school and my teachers were important to me.

I didn't see myself as a student but I did get into the University of California and later Stanford University graduate school. —Bev

Naomi's Voice

I became hidden to keep bad things from happening to me. As a young child I was loving and sensitive as well as easily bruised and shy. My first seven years were like paradise. At seven my mother had a breakdown, however, and my father's job that he was proud of ended. My mother was hospitalized when I was about ten. My father, a 5-Observer, was ashamed and embarrassed and didn't talk about any of it. He was a drinker but I didn't know it. At the time my parents were frustrated, angry, sorrowing, and tense. My 4-Romantic mother was probably bipolar and extraverted while I was introverted. She had lots of parties, which was difficult for me because I was so private, but I wanted connection deeply. The atmosphere, which had been loving before, became a war zone.

Mother hospitalized; everything changed

I mourned the loss of my previously loving mother, who had been attentive to me. When she came back from the hospital something changed. Her shyness and softness was beaten out of her.

My mother's image was important to her. She felt threatened and didn't know how to handle me becoming different from her. She thought I owed it to her to have the same tastes she had and she fought with me about what I wore. We had battles practically to the death. She must have felt I was abandoning her, as though her life was at stake, when I became myself. She liked to wear black and red and white and I didn't. I wanted to hide and wear things where I'd feel safe—dark coats, navy blue, brown, and black. Our coloring was different. I was blond with blue eyes. She was a brunette with brown eyes.

Numb and lonely

I looked different on the outside from how I felt inside. I felt different from what was around me. There didn't seem to be a place for me in my family so I numbed myself—I don't know if it was conscious or not. It was like there was a clay casing over me. I was lonely but I tried to toughen myself and bypass how I felt. I'd say, "I can take this," but sometimes I couldn't and felt lost.

My music was private

A lot of the time I was in a battle with my mother. Loving to sing and make up songs came from a private place in me. My mother couldn't sing, so she felt my voice "belonged" to her and she had a right to tell me what to do with it. Around 15, when we lived in New York City, I had a guitar. One time she asked me to play and sing at one of her parties and I said I'd rather not. She called me into the kitchen, got irate and livid, and guilt-tripped me into doing it. I felt so beat down I sang the song for her friends. But I knew I wasn't really there, and that agreeing to sing against my will was a violation. That was scary. Afterwards, I felt I couldn't trust myself since I did it without wanting to. Since I didn't have a voice about whether to share my voice, my ability to sing in front of other people shut down. I stopped singing. Something had been stolen from me.

I wish a voice in me had said, "You're entitled to your life, don't abandon it. Sometimes your parents will make you do things you don't want to do, things that violate your private self. Do your best to know your private self is precious and try to keep it for yourself." Looking back, I would have told myself not to sing that day and found a way to say what I needed to say. I would have written in a journal. I would have said no to those people and to doing things that violated me. "I hope you understand. I don't feel like singing."

I made my mother the "bad guy," and my father the "good guy." I gave my father a vial of marijuana when I was 17 or 18. He liked it. I didn't know he was an alcoholic. —Naomi

Part III: The Peace Seeker and the Seven Goals

I'm always ambivalent.
Most of the time, that is.

1. **Developing the habit of doing homework and tasks regularly**. Notice how your 1-Perfectionist wing models the ability to work and get things finished.

2. **Being mindful of your body**—your health, appearance, and exercise. 9's often find it pleasurable to swing, swim, or hang out in nature.

3. **Peace Seekers are often generous and kind friends.** Since you don't like conflict, try not to show anger passive/aggressively, as in

this burger cartoon, but strive to be direct:

4. **You are already likely to be mindful of your emotional/ spiritual development.** Peace Seekers often have a natural leaning toward the spiritual. You may be attracted to nature and find solace

there.

5. **Nurturing your intellect.** You have the ability to see many sides to an issue and you may have a gift for synthesizing information.

Your Learning Style

- Peace Seekers tend to be feeling types, like to be flexible, and to focus on possibilities for people. Some, however, are more structured and want to control their environment. Peace Seekers have a wide range of traits.
- When you study with others, make sure you give and receive positive feedback.
- Don't take criticism or feedback personally.
- Make an effort to evaluate how much you like or don't like the subjects you study in school as a way to develop the ability to make decisions about yourself.
- Make sure you have a comfortable learning environment to study in.

6. **Developing interests based on your passions and values.** Peace Seekers are often interested in how people live in other cultures, too.

7. **Educating yourself on career choices** that incorporate your innate strengths, which include being adaptable and open, having a broad perspective, and the ability to listen. If these strengths differ from your passions (see #6), develop them both. Your passions will feed your soul while your strengths can support you financially.

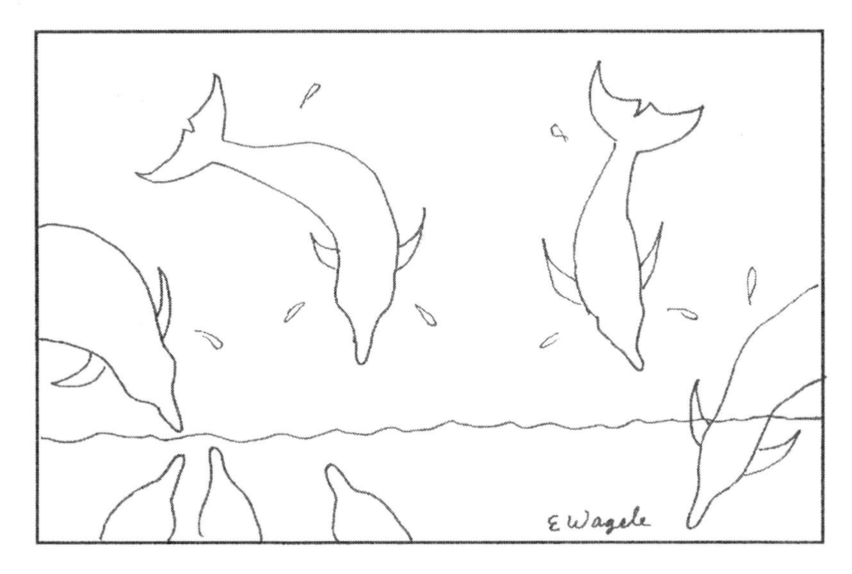

Connecting and exchanging information.

Part IV: What I Like about being a Peace Seeker

Part V: Healing Words for Peace Seekers

The basis of peace and stability, in any society, has to be the fullest respect for the human rights of all its people. —John Hume

We can never obtain peace in the outer world until we make peace with ourselves. —Dalai Lama

A leader is best when people barely know he exists, when his work is done, his aim fulfilled, they will say: we did it ourselves.—Lao Tzu

The Enneagram of Shoes
???
1. The Teacher
2. The Healer
3. The Dresser
4. The Artist
5. The Thinker
6. What if... ?
7. The Trekking Model
8. The Viking
9. The Nature Model

Chapter 10 - Developing Leadership Using the Enneagram

Leadership is unlocking people's potential to do better. —Bill Bradley

The Enneagram can help you become a flexible and successful leader. Along with learning your own and others' types, it teaches you to perceive your natural strengths and be more confident of using them. It also teaches you to identify which skills you could improve. The best leaders provide good examples that others want to follow. Good teachers lead by inspiring their students to learn. Good leaders in sports, clubs, and businesses inspire their teams to cooperate on achieving a common goal.

Trusting the leader's ability to lead helps followers perform well. Important leadership qualities include knowing when to assume control and when to let go of control.

Successful leaders:

- Communicate a vision and initiate change
- Instill pride, respect, and trust
- Perceive others' behaviors and potentials—and understand and accept ways of being not like their own.
- Encourage both cooperation and healthy conflict
- Generate enthusiasm

In some countries, consensus is the preferred way of leading. Switzerland, for example, is led by seven people. The seven then elect a president who can break ties.

Leadership Quiz

In order to become a well-rounded leader, evaluate your strengths by answering the following questions YES or NO, then rate all the questions you answered "yes" to according to which are your strongest and weakest:

1. Do you inspire by your high principles and work ethic?

Yes__ No__

Perfectionists' incentives to lead include making the world a better place.

2. Do you encourage by creating an atmosphere of harmony and caring?

Yes__ No__

Helpers' incentives to lead include helping others succeed.

3. Do you inspire with your team spirit and willingness to work hard?

Yes__ No__

Achievers' incentives to lead include the challenge of pursuing an ambitious goal and getting the job done efficiently.

4. Do your compassion and unusual way of seeing things inspire people?

Yes__ No__

Romantics' incentives to lead include the desire to produce something meaningful to them, such as beauty.

5. Do you influence others to be curious and to want to learn, like you do?

Yes__ No__

Observers' incentives to lead include seeking enjoyment in the learning process and in the work itself.

6. Do your alertness and loyalty to the group inspire people?

Yes__ No__

Questioners' incentives to lead include fulfilling ideals, such as helping the underdog and improving security.

7. Do you generate enthusiasm and excel at persuasion?

Yes__ No__

Adventurers' incentives to lead include keeping things exciting and fun.

8. Do you exude a sense of confidence that others respect?

Yes__ No__

Asserters' incentives to lead include seeking truth, promoting justice, and protecting others.

9. Do you dislike conflict and try to build agreement?

Yes__ No__

Peace Seekers' incentives to lead include keeping or creating peace and promoting community.

Use your best strengths and skills to lead. Develop other leadership abilities by emulating the types that are strong in what you lack.

The Nine Types of Leaders and Their Strengths

Perfectionists as leaders:

- Are clear about the standards they want their team to follow and make precise, detailed plans
- Notice who participates and who works hard
- Try to be conscientious examples that workers will want to follow

How to develop leadership strengths similar to the Perfectionist's

Perfectionists make use of their strong morals, ethics, and high standards when leading. They try hard to avoid mistakes. If you want to develop strengths Perfectionists have naturally, work on being well-organized and structured. Make plans with clear guidelines and supervise others in carrying them out. Be the first to start work on a project and the last to quit

STORY

A Perfectionist teen noticed graffiti on the fence of one of the churches near her. She asked the pastor if she and a group of friends could clean it up, then did research to find out how best to remove it. They spent two weekends scrubbing the fence, and cleaned up well after themselves.

Leadership is an interactive conversation that pulls people toward becoming comfortable with the language of personal responsibility and commitment. —John G. Agno

Helpers as leaders:

- Discover, use, and praise the special talents of each person on their team
- Interact personally with their team and tend to minimize paperwork
- May lead indirectly and encourage others to take the most visible roles

How to develop leadership strengths similar to the Helper's

Helpers naturally please and support others, create a warm atmosphere, and understand what others need. If you want to develop these people-oriented strengths, be empathic and determine the assets of those on your team. Perform beyond the call of duty.

STORY

A Helper teen wanted to do something for a neighbor who was sick and couldn't go out. She called a meeting of neighbors, making sure everyone felt comfortable, and included a treat as a reward for coming. Then she signed them up to bring the neighbor lady food, clean her house, and work in her garden until she could manage on her own.

Communication is the real work of leadership. —Nitin Nohria

Achievers as leaders:

- Are competitive, enthusiastic, ambitious, and optimistic
- Work quickly to get the job done once they have their goal in mind
- Strive for practical, successful results that look good to others

How to develop leadership strengths similar to the Achiever's

Achievers are naturally productive and enjoy competition and performing. They motivate members to transcend their own self-interests for the sake of the team. If you want to develop the strengths 3's have, work on being optimistic, charging ahead, and your ability to compete. Be practical and keep your eyes on the prize until you get your mission accomplished.

STORY

An Achiever teen read about starving children in Africa and wanted to raise money to buy them food. He persuaded his friends to help him put on a car wash, first lining up a parking lot that had access to water. He took charge of advertising it and making posters. They raised enough money to feed 100 children for four or five months.

The only real training for leadership is leadership. —Anthony Jay

Romantics as leaders:

- Are compassionate and arrange team members into compatible groups
- Stay emotionally engaged
- Are creative and discerning. They encourage their team to do distinctive work and avoid the routine in favor of a unique approach

How to develop leadership strengths similar to the Romantic's

Romantics are naturally emotionally sensitive and have artistic temperaments. They prefer to work on projects that are meaningful to them. If you want to develop strengths Romantics have, appreciate others' pain and tune in to the poetic and artistic side of life. Express yourself and find special ways to present your ideas.

STORY

A Romantic teen was upset that there was homeless family sleeping outdoors in her neighborhood. The children didn't appear to be going to school. She got some friends together and they called social services and school and city government officials to get the family counseling and a place to live. Because the teens fought for them, the family was able to move into an apartment and the children started attending school.

Leadership is much more an art, a belief, a condition of the heart than a set of things to do. —Max Depree

Observers as leaders:

- Encourage their team members to work independently
- Focus on important ideas they want to work on more than on how their team members relate to each other
- Are thoughtful, research-oriented, and examine all angles of an issue before making a decision

How to develop leadership strengths similar to the Observer's

Observers readily analyze problems and bring their objectivity to a project. They may prefer leading and working behind the scenes and communicating non-verbally. If you want to develop the strengths Observers have naturally, become interested in learning, make sure of your facts, and explore the ins and outs of your project in depth.

STORY

A teacher asked an Observer teen to head a team learning to do research and write a history paper. The Observer divided the research subtopics among them and gave them a deadline for submitting what they found. He wanted to write up the final paper himself, however, to be sure the information was clearly presented.

Leadership is the wise use of power. Power is the intention to translate intention into reality and sustain it. —Warren G. Bennis

Questioners as leaders:

- Encourage loyalty of team members and are loyal themselves
- Focus on what could go wrong and take quick action when they find a problem
- Are watchful and protect the team members from any abuse from outside

How to develop leadership strengths similar to the Questioner's

If you want to develop the strengths Questioners have naturally, take a skeptical look at the issues and be safety-conscious. Questioners want to be certain of their responsibilities and often excel under pressure. They can expend a tremendous amount of energy on their tasks, are good at troubleshooting, and are loyal to the team.

STORY

A Questioner teen noticed the railing of a bridge across a creek in her neighborhood was falling apart. Not only did it look bad, it was also dangerous. Somebody might get hurt by falling on the sharp rocks below. She called experts to see what the bridge would need to become absolutely safe, made out a schedule and a list of duties, and asked some of her friends to join her in fixing it.

Leadership has been defined as the power to hide your panic from others.—Lau Tzu

Adventurers as leaders:

- Are charming, enthusiastic, and convey a cheerful attitude to team members
- Act quickly and have confidence in their plans
- Spread the power out so one person isn't responsible for everything

How to develop leadership strengths similar to the Adventurer's

If you want to develop the strengths Adventurers have naturally, work on being optimistic and curious. Adventurers like new experiences, want to have fun, and are good at networking. They like to keep moving and doing a variety of jobs.

STORY

When an Adventurer teen went to a new school, she wanted to stay in touch with her friends from her old school so she decided to network. She started a group on Facebook and asked everyone in her former class to join. If they didn't join within a week of asking them, she would try to persuade them with a phone call. Nearly the whole class joined up.

The very essence of leadership is that you have to have a vision. You can't blow an uncertain trumpet. —Theodore Hesburgh

Asserters as leaders:

- Are energetic, confident, and protective of team members
- Encourage openness and find out where the team members stand
- Are direct and bold

How to develop leadership strengths similar to the Asserter's

If you want to develop the strengths Asserters have naturally, work on protecting others, standing up for the truth, and taking charge when a leader is needed. Asserters are dynamic and competitive. They tell you what they think and they want to hear the truth. They are not afraid of expressing anger.

STORY

An Asserter teen happened upon a bully who was threatening one of the other students. Instead of calling for help, he let his full anger loose on the bully verbally. It worked. The bully thought twice about bothering other kids after that. Word spread among the other students of how the Asserter had protected the kid who needed help. The Asserter became a respected leader in the school and his example helped decrease the cases of bullying.

I forgot to shake hands and be friendly. It was an important lesson about leadership. —Lee Iacocca

Peace Seekers as leaders:

- Are generous and establish friendly relationships with team members
- Ask for recommendations from all the members and share the credit
- Look at the big picture

How to develop leadership strengths similar to the Peace Seeker's

Peace Seekers are good at seeing how the different parts of a project fit together. If you want to develop the strengths Peace Seekers have naturally, look at all sides of an issue, work on your mediating skills, and avoid conflict. Keep things pleasant, work for a consensus, and accept your team members for who they are.

STORY

A Peace Seeker teen noticed the city had plans to cut down some beautiful old trees in her neighborhood in order to build a shopping center. First, she checked with a tree expert and found out the trees were healthy. Then she called a meeting of some friends and told them she thought the builders could avoid cutting down most of the trees. Her group got people to sign petitions and called the mayor and the city counsel, which saved the trees.

Leadership has a harder job to do than just choose sides. It must bring sides together. —Jesse Jackson

Conclusion

The Enneagram encourages you to evaluate your own performance, to express who you are, and to search for positive possibilities. By participating in an accomplishment, you increase your connection to the community and your self-worth, and you enhance your personal identity. Being linked to social collectives successfully adds meaning to your life and encourages you to seek out more opportunities to lead and to serve.

Young people can sometimes accomplish more than adults when it comes to handling their own problems. In Canada, for example, the federal government financed a program to train 2,400 people ages 13-17. These teen leaders delivered workshops on bullying to at least 20 people each—50,000 altogether. Youth-led forums in many parts of Canada aim to create a cadre of youth who are willing to stand up to bullies.

Appendix I

Drawing Exercise for Hope and Healing

This tool is useful for helping you change behaviors and attitudes and for transforming upsetting memories. You can use it throughout your life.

1. Write down something that has bothered you a lot—something you did or something someone else did to you.
2. Now draw a picture of it.
3. Think about how you wish this event had been different.
4. Draw another picture changing this scene into a positive one.

Now your brain has two memories: the real event and the positive wish-version you drew of it. Drawing the two versions helps you react differently under similar circumstances or change your behavior. Repeat this exercise whenever you need to change your perspective.

Here is another use of this exercise. If you have a problem (drug or alcohol use by you or someone close to you, someone threatening or bullying you, or other problems at home, at school, or in your neighborhood), perhaps you'd like to tell someone who can help you—your guidance counselor, your parents, or your pastor. Instead of keeping it a secret, use this tool to practice what you want to say, and then take action.

A journey of a thousand miles begins with a single step. —Lao Tzu

Appendix II Resources for Adolescents

If you or someone you know is in immediate danger of harming themselves or others, or of being harmed, or for a medical emergency, call 911 first. If you're not sure whether your situation is an emergency, call 911. If you have an urgent problem or want to vent, search online for *Hotline for teens* to find help where you live or use one of the following:

This website has information on many issues:
Hotlines For Troubled Teens http://www.ehow.com/about_4761425_hotlines-troubled teens.html

Also

Bullying and cyber bullying

"Stomp Out Bullying":

http://www.pacerteensagainstbullying.org/#/home

Bullying statistics:

http://www.covenanteyes.com/2012/01/17/bullying-statistics-fast-facts-about-cyberbullying/

Depression

http://www.medicinenet.com/teen_depression/article.htm
http://www.universityhealthsystem.com/myths-and-facts/

Drinking

http://www.cdc.gov/alcohol/fact-sheets/underage-drinking.htm
http://www.centurycouncil.org/underage-drinking/statistics

Gangs

http://www.helpinggangyouth.com/statistics.html

Marijuana

http://teens.drugabuse.gov/drug-facts/marijuana

Need Treatment? 1-800-662-HELP

http://www.nih.gov/news/health/dec2012/nida-19.htm

Mental illness and drug abuse

http://www.aacap.org/cs/root/resources_for_families/child_and_adolescent_mental_illness_statistics

Obsessive-compulsive disorder

http://medicalcenter.osu.edu/patientcare/healthcare_services/mental_health/mental_health_about/obsessive_compulsive_disorder/Pages/index.aspx

Panic disorder

http://medicalcenter.osu.edu/patientcare/healthcare_services/mental_health/mental_health_about/panic_disorder/Pages/index.aspx

Physical and emotional abuse

http://www.focusas.com/Abuse-Physical.html
http://kidshealth.org/teen/your_mind/families/family_abuse.html

PTSD (post-traumatic stress)

http://www.ptsd.va.gov/public/pages/ptsd-children-adolescents.asp

Pregnancy and sex

http://www.guttmacher.org/pubs/FB-ATSRH.html

Self-injury (cutting etc.)

http://www.healthyplace.com/abuse/self-injury/self-injury-self-harm-statistics-and-facts/

Sexual orientation and other issues hotline

http://crisislink.org/crisislink-services/crisislink-hotlines/

Suicide

Hotlines:

1.800.273.TALK (8255)
http://www.suicide.org/teen-suicide-and-youth-suicide.html

Article:

http://medicalcenter.osu.edu/patientcare/healthcare_services/mental_health/mental_health_about/children/suicide/Pages/index.aspx

Acknowledgments

Elizabeth would like to thank the following people for their help with this book:

Hap Allen
James Campbell
Joyce Chang
Tom C. Clark
Helen Clarkson
Brian Conlon
Jan Conlon
Mary Beth Crenna
Kimberly Fink
Jaki Girdner
Bev Hansen
Thea Kelley
Dr. Kim Hwan-Young
Ernie Kotlier
Pamela Lund
Charlotte McDaniel
Bob Levin
Diane Mintz
Susan Overton
Sara Reed
Naomi Rose
Elayne Savage
Anne Shapiro
Alan Sheets
Jeanne St. John
Ingrid Stabb
Vicki Tam
Ron Tompkins
Revan Tranter
Don Villa
Gus Wagele
Nick Wagele

About the Author

Elizabeth Wagele (pronounced "Way'-glee") attended the University of California at Berkeley majoring in music and music composition and raised four children with her husband Gus. She has co-written *The Enneagram Made Easy*, *Are You My Type, Am I Yours?* (these two with co-author Renee Baron) and *The Career Within You* (with co-author Ingrid Stabb). She has written *The Enneagram of Parenting*, *Finding the Birthday Cake*, *The Happy Introvert—a Wild and Crazy Guide for Finding Your True Self*, and *The Enneagram of Death*. In her *Beethoven Enneagram* CD she plays excerpts of Beethoven sonatas with narration.

Wagele books, cartoons, essays, reviews, and blog: wagele.com

Wagele Psychology Today blog: http://bit.ly/psychtdy

CPSIA information can be obtained
at www.ICGtesting.com
Printed in the USA
BVOW00s0540051116
466705BV00004B/33/P